WITH THE FIFTH ARMY AIR FORCE

WITH THE Fifth Army Air Force

PHOTOS FROM THE PACIFIC THEATER

James P. Gallagher

FOREWORD BY Eric Bergerud

THE JOHNS HOPKINS UNIVERSITY PRESS
BALTIMORE AND LONDON

© 2001 The Johns Hopkins University Press
All rights reserved. Published 2001
Printed in Italy on acid-free paper

9 8 7 6 5 4 3 2 1

The Johns Hopkins University Press
2715 North Charles Street
Baltimore, Maryland 21218-4363
www.press.jhu.edu

FRONTISPIECE
A P-38 in dispersal at Dobodura.

LIBRARY OF CONGRESS
CATALOGING-IN-PUBLICATION DATA

Gallagher, James P., 1920–
    With the Fifth Army Air Force : photos from the
Pacific Theater / James P. Gallagher ; foreword by
Eric Bergerud.
        p.   cm.
ISBN 0-8018-6849-1 (hardcover : alk. paper)
    1. Gallagher, James P., 1920– 2. World War, 1939–
1945—Personal narratives, American. 3. United
States. Army Air Forces—Biography. 4. United
States. Army Air Forces. Air Force, 5th—Pictorial
works. 5. World War, 1939–1945—Campaigns—
Pacific Ocean—Pictorial works. 6. World War,
1939–1945—Campaigns—Japan—Pictorial works.
7. World War, 1939–1945—Photography. I. Title.
D811.G29 A3 2002
940.54'26 — dc21   2001003732

A catalog record for this book is available
from the British Library.

CONTENTS

vii   Foreword, *by Eric Bergerud*

xvii   Preface

xxi   Acknowledgments

3   To Milne Bay, New Guinea

18   Oro Bay / Dobodura, New Guinea

38   Cape Gloucester, New Britain

65   Sansapor and Middelburg, New Guinea

83   To Leyte, with the 49th Fighter Group

102   Lingayen Gulf

126   Motobu, Okinawa

139   Touchdown at Atsugi

163   Epilogue

167   Index

Occasionally, Gallagher could take a break from his wartime duties and just admire a sunset, like this one off Milne Bay.

FOREWORD

James Gallagher's World War II memoir is a splendid look, in both words and photographs, at the war in the Pacific, an often overlooked theater of history's largest and most important war. Gallagher gives the modern reader a fascinating examination of what that war looked like to one man who helped fight it. He intentionally avoids constructing another narrative history of events as seen by generals and admirals. This was a wise decision. Those in the midst of conflict rarely appreciate the big picture: war for most men is what takes place in their own backyard. Gallagher captures the view from the bottom of the fishbowl.

The campaign in which Gallagher served was a large and significant one, although it is often overshadowed in historical literature by the titanic struggle in Europe. The reader, therefore, might gain something more from this excellent book if given an overview of the military situation in which it is set.

While Gallagher was a young college student, great events took place that shaped the direction and duration of his later journey. In December 1941 Tokyo undertook an audacious move to establish a maritime empire in Asian waters. The primary target was Southeast Asia, especially the Dutch East Indies, which possessed natural resources such as oil and rubber that would, the Japanese hoped, allow them to create an industrial state to rival any in the world. Gaining this prize required war against the then imperial masters of the region, Great Britain and Holland, both beleaguered by Hitler's legions. The United States, then in possession of the Philippines and with powerful forces not committed in Europe, was seen as the most powerful potential enemy by Japan.

The result was the attack on Pearl Harbor and an amphibious blitzkrieg throughout Pacific waters. By June 1942, Japanese forces had startled the world, conquering Burma, Malaya, the Dutch East Indies (present-day Indonesia), the Philippines, and island outposts as far-flung as New Britain, near Australia, and Wake Island, uncomfortably close to the Hawaiian Islands. Japanese land, air, and naval forces swept everything before them and appeared invincible. Fortunately for the United States, the Japanese navy rolled the dice one time too often and came to grief at Midway. The spectacular American triumph at Midway stopped Tokyo's expansion. The United States was, however, still left with the daunting task of advancing over thousands of miles of territory to reverse the gains won by the early Japanese juggernaut. When put on the defensive, Tokyo decided to create a line of maritime strong points with powerful air units, supported by the still strong Japanese fleet, which would prove impervious to attack. The Americans, Tokyo hoped, would see the enormous costs necessary to break the Imperial Pacific line and accept a compromise peace favorable to Japan.

Although it was beginning a massive war in Europe, Washington decided to engage Japan seriously early in the war. At first the goal was defensive, preventing the Japanese from attacking or isolating Australia. To organize this effort, General Douglas MacArthur was ordered out of the Philippines and given command of American and Australian forces. Soon a hotly contested campaign was underway for the strategically vital island of New Guinea. After victory at Midway, the United States also decided that a limited counterattack against Japanese positions northeast of Australia was possible. The result was the invasion of Guadalcanal in the Solomon Islands. Perilous moments occurred in both areas (geographically close, by Pacific standards), but Allied forces triumphed in both eastern New Guinea and Guadalcanal. By the end of 1943, the U.S. Navy began launching a massive fleet of new warships, supported by a greatly expanded U.S. Marine amphibious force. This armada was to drive directly from Hawaii toward Japan.

Consequently, when James Gallagher arrived in New Guinea, the United States, ably assisted by Australia, was poised to strike the Japanese defensive line. In theory, the drive through the Central Pacific would get the Americans close to Japan quickly, but it offered few bases for a staged advance. Targets available were small islands that threatened terrible casualties for the attackers. A thrust from New Guinea would get the Americans more quickly into the East Indies or the Philippines, objectives that, if seized, would cripple Japan's ability to make war. With more and larger islands in MacArthur's theater, the Americans could make better use of their superior firepower and mobility. After much argument, Washington decided that resources were available to attack Japan from both directions. This tactic strained the enemy. Not knowing where to expect attack, the Japanese flung their military resources throughout the Pacific, preventing a concentrated defense against either line of attack.

Like many bright young men, James Gallagher joined the U.S. Army Air Force. (The independent U.S. Air Force was not created until after World War II.) This decision, although Gallagher did not anticipate it at the time, put him under MacArthur in New Guinea. This was no accident. No conflict in history was more dependent upon air power than the struggle between the United States and Japan. It is vital to realize that the Pacific war was an island war. No island, including Japan, is able to sustain a war effort unless supported by supplies from the outside. This was especially true in the South and Southwest Pacific, where the islands were barren of resources and both sides were dependent upon supply from the outside for operations of any kind. This meant that control of sea lanes meant control of the battlefield. In practice, control of the sea lanes depended upon air superiority. As illustrated at Pearl Harbor and Midway, and reinforced by countless other examples in the Pacific, a warship could move under enemy air power only at the greatest risk. Supply ships were hopelessly vulnerable to air attack. The military equation in the Pacific was simple. If one side gained air superiority, it could isolate its enemy. This would give the ascendant force the ability to bypass enemy garrisons, assault the foe with merciless air attacks, or both. Once air supremacy was gained, almost any military feat was possible. Without air power, one could do nothing but wait for starvation or destruction.

No leader in the Pacific war was more dedicated to the use of air power than Douglas MacArthur. One of the general's earliest command reorganizations led to the creation of the USAAF Fifth Air Force, under the redoubtable General George Kenney. Although he started with meager capabilities, Kenney was able to cajole Washington into slowly increasing his supply of aircraft and men. From the first, Kenney drove the Fifth Air Force hard. Many of his units were undoubtedly pushed to the point of diminishing returns. In any event, Kenney and the officers around him relished their "throw away the book" attitude. By late 1942, Fifth Air Force engineers were making field modifications on their aircraft that confounded the manufacturers but made the planes far better weapons for the strange theater they were assigned to. Within a short time the Fifth Air Force established a reputation of brutal effectiveness. Their aircrews, often operating on a shoestring, cultivated a kind of swashbuckler attitude. Kenney and MacArthur combined to help create amazing victories in New Guinea from 1943 to early 1944. In June 1944 the Pentagon combined the Fifth Air Force

with the Thirteenth Air Force, which had aided the marines and the navy in the Solomons, to form the Far Eastern Air Force (FEAF). Regardless of the change in organizational charts, the airmen of both air forces maintained their original identity. Gallagher was a member of the Fifth Air Force, period.

That unit was entirely land based. The public today associates the Pacific war with aircraft carriers. The association has foundation. Throughout much of 1942, the carrier forces of both sides determined the shape of operations. By late 1942, however, the United States and Japan had lost most of their pre–Pearl Harbor carriers and kept the few survivors in reserve. Between October 1942 and June 1944, carrier-borne aircraft played a minor role in the Pacific war. (In the last year of the war, the massive U.S. fleet expansion allowed the carriers to once again become dominant—but only on the American side.) When the conflict centered on New Guinea and the Solomons, therefore, the air war was between land-based units. The Japanese fielded a formidable force at their great base at Rabaul in New Britain and at large fields in New Guinea. The Allies countered with marine, army, and New Zealand aircraft in the Solomons. In New Guinea the Fifth Air Force included a sizable and effective Australian contingent.

The land-based air war differed greatly from the carrier engagements. While carriers would maneuver for a heart-stopping series of strikes, land bases could slug it out for months on end. This allowed the maximum use of every type of aircraft. Heavy bombers of the Fifth Air Force attacked enemy airfields and shipping lanes while keeping a keen eye out for Japanese ship movements. The feared Fifth Air Force "strafers" (modified b-25s with 12.50-caliber machine guns firing forward) mauled shipping lanes and devastated airfields with a blizzard of small bombs dropped with tiny parachutes (the famous "parafrag," a newly coined term often attributed to Kenney

himself). Flying cover were the fighter squadrons of the Fifth Air Force. Because they were in action so often, the best pilots of Kenney's pirates became some of the greatest American aces in World War II. America's "ace of aces" was Richard Bong, with forty kills. Other Fifth Air Force pilots, such as Thomas McGuire, Charles MacDonald, Jerry Johnson, and Robert De-Haven, accumulated impressive claims and led their units to one victory after another. A visit from the Fifth Air Force was very bad news for the Japanese.

Much of this was observed by James Gallagher, who was not a pilot but a member of a control squadron and, later, an communications officer. His duties highlight one of the oddities of the air war in the Pacific. Although operating in some of the most primitive areas on earth, Gallagher was a part of a highly sophisticated war machine. He dealt with radar, radio signals, and other information to keep track of what was going on with large numbers of aircraft—both friendly and enemy.

Gallagher had challenging and no doubt interesting duty. His job was also undertaken under conditions that most people today would find hideous. The South and Southwest Pacific area was very sparsely populated, and for good reason. It was home to a vicious climate and every germ known to medicine — and many that were not — in 1942. Anyone in the South Pacific lived in a region where the temperature often stood at 100 degrees and the humidity at near 100 percent. Rain and mud were always present. Often the heat was so intense that early morning mud would transform into dust by the time of takeoff. Everyone in the area was highly vulnerable to malaria, dengue fever, dysentery, and "jungle rot." Gallagher was at both Milne Bay and Cape Gloucester, two sites often singled out as particularly miserable places in a miserable area.

Gallagher was part of the huge number of support personnel required to keep the Pacific war moving. Because the military had to create the most elementary infrastructure and supply huge numbers of men, the "rear" in the Pacific was larger than anywhere else. In the meantime, ground personnel in an air unit faced a different situation than many of their comrades in rear services. The Japanese either harassed or attacked American air bases regularly. Therefore men like Gallagher received frequent visits from serious air attack or small night raids. Air bases were tiny targets compared to a city, so the ratio of bombs dropped per square yard of inhabited territory was a serious matter for those on the receiving end. Gallagher was at air bases throughout his service, and thus he was under fire on numerous occasions. Being a cook in England would have been easier.

Gallagher saw enemy action directed at him, and he also saw Fifth Air Force units going in the other direction. For the last year of the war, he was part of the 49th Fighter Group, perhaps the most distinguished unit of its type flying under army colors in the entire

Pacific war. After a distinguished record in New Guinea, the group fought from Tacloban field on Leyte in one of the last and most important battles fought by the Fifth Air Force. It was only fitting, as Gallagher describes, that aircraft from the 49th were the first to land in Japan after surrender.

In my own books, I have tried to describe the efforts of thousands of men supporting or flying several hundred combat aircraft. Yet the war was fought by individuals organized, for the most part, into quite small groups. Gallagher's book provides an account of what service was like, day by day, in the vortex of history's great storm. By rights, a young man from Loyola College would not have ended up at Tacloban, via Milne Bay, Cape Gloucester, Hollandia, and other places at the edge of the planet. (As Gallagher points out, a tour with the Fifth was a reeducation of the tongue; he had to learn the names of Dobodura, Gili Gili, Lae, Rabaul, Sanananda, Soputa, Buna, and Tsili Tsili, among others.)

Because of the massive force of World War II, young Gallagher was thrust to the "end of the earth" as part of a highly sophisticated military machine. He also had a camera. World War II was not a "snapshot" war. Military photographers took spectacular photos of battle, while those servicemen with usually humble cameras took group photos. What is often lost between the grand scenes of battle and group shots of the guys in the squad is a visual record of the war as it actually took place.

Gallagher produces this record wonderfully. There are scenes of air bases, where all USAAF personnel spent the vast percentage of their time. Some of the ugly side of service in the tropics is reproduced. (Read on if you want to compare the size of a South Pacific bug relative to a cigarette pack.) Like everyone else doing his job in 1944, Gallagher dealt with the navy and long-distance voyages. A sea voyage in the Pacific was restful and boring. It could also be tense and violent.

Any real fan of World War II aviation will appreciate Gallagher's photos. During his service, Gallagher came into contact with almost every famous unit of the Fifth Air Force. He has pictures of the 90th Bomber Group (the Jolly Rogers), the 475th Fighter Group (commanded by the brilliant tactician Charles MacDonald), plus his own 49th Fighter Group. Aircraft photographed, very well, include the major planes in the Pacific, such as the P-38, P-40, P-47, B-24, and B-25. But there was an avalanche of aircraft in the theater, and Gallagher picks up the odd ones as well: a B-26 of the Silver Fleet, an A-24, a Supermarine Walrus, a Black Widow, an Australian Mosquito, a late-war A-26 Invader, and a Tigercat. Gallagher even encountered a fighter from the Mexican Expeditionary Air Force. His photos of Japanese aircraft will also interest aircraft enthusiasts.

The photos show planes the way they really looked. Familiar photos of World War II aircraft in the air show sleek, beautiful, and deadly machines.

They were that. But Gallagher's shots show another side of reality. The planes he dealt with daily and often photographed were worn, scratched, and dented. Planes that in today's Air Force would be junked instantly soldiered on. There was a war to be won.

As much as I like Gallagher's photos, I am partial to his economical and elegant prose in text and captions. The author recaptures much of what I conceive as the essence of the war. The straightforward narrative captures wonderfully the "start and stop" tempo of the Pacific war. The author also reproduces choice examples of the dry and dark wit so characteristic of the irreverent American servicemen. (Who else would call the LST landing ships "long slow targets"? Other examples abound.) Air operations took place with great speed, and so did tragedy. It is fitting that the author's account has a hard edge. Men die and aircraft are destroyed in battle. They are also lost because of friendly fire and accidents. Some men die of youthful stupidity.

Gallagher also captures some of the utter strangeness of war. A section of beautiful Japanese fighters flying "on the deck" over Tacloban inexplicably brings no fire from either side. For three years, James Gallagher's life was not business as usual.

The author lived in a world of very large numbers of very young men very far from home. All were involved in action antithetical to the rhythm of civilian life. Most, like Gallagher, wanted to return from the helter-skelter of World War II to a world of peace. And so they did, but only after victory. Anyone interested in a vivid depiction of a world far away in time and place from ours will appreciate this book. The appreciation can only increase knowing these events continue to shape the world we live in.

ERIC BERGERUD

PREFACE

Books on the so-called big picture of
World War II are plentiful enough.
They grace coffee tables and fill many a
shelf in American dens. Far less ambitious, the photos and text that follow
make up a photographic memoir, a
recollection of one citizen's experience
between 1943 and 1945 while serving
with the Fifth Army Air Force in New
Guinea, New Britain, the Philippines,
Okinawa, and the conquered Japanese
homeland. I have included here a few
action scenes of United States air
attacks on Japanese targets, especially
airfields. Some of them, to the best of
my knowledge, have never before been
published, and the viewer may find

much of interest in them. But I want this book to enter in the record some images that are less familiar to students of the war—aircraft in the field, landing strips cut out of the jungle, the equipment essential to air operations—and to provide a glimpse of the day-to-day life many of us shared. Needless to add, I want this appended documentary evidence to pay tribute to the men who were with me then, especially to those who lost their lives during that long campaign, so long ago.

All of us in my generation found ourselves caught up, one way or another and not exactly by surprise, in World War II. In 1940, then twenty years old, I was a student at Loyola College in my hometown of Baltimore, Maryland. Upon graduating in June of 1942, my friends and I did not hesitate to answer the country's call. Enlisting in the Army Air Force, I selected communications as my military occupational specialty (I had learned a good deal on that subject from my dad, whose hobby was short-

wave broadcasting). Soon assigned as a cadet in AAF communications officer training, I received second lieutenant's bars in March 1943. Practical training followed with fighter squadrons at Richmond, Virginia, and at Camp Springs Army Air Field, Maryland, near Washington, D.C. In June I received orders to the 33d Fighter Control Squadron, with headquarters in Philadelphia. The 33d, with its radio network, was an integral part of the East Coast's air defense system.

In the late summer of 1943, the 33d FCS ceased routine operations and withdrew from what was then known as the Philadelphia Air Defense Wing. The squadron moved to Dundalk, Maryland, near Baltimore, as its assembly, or staging, point. Then in September 1943, headquarters ordered us to travel at a "specified time" by rail to Camp Patrick Henry, Virginia, to arrive on September 25, 1943, at 2000 hours (8 p.m.). The orders referred cryptically to a classified letter from the commander, Hampton Roads Port of Embarka-

A friend snapped this shot of me just a couple of days after the arrival of the 33d.

tion, Newport News, Virginia, the directives in which we were to have "complied with." The handwriting was clearly on the wall; we were headed overseas, to a still-unknown destination.

Besides my issued military equipment and a few personal belongings, I had with me a Baldaxette camera, a pretty good one, and four or five rolls of 120-millimeter film. While in high school I had taken up photography—developing, printing, and enlarging my own work—and at Loyola I had worked as staff photographer for the student newspaper, the *Greyhound*. I had a vague intention of eventually putting together a scrapbook of my overseas tour. This idea may seem strange or unlikely: cameras and photographs were strictly prohibited at stateside Army Air Force operating fields in those days, and when troops embarked for service abroad the army impounded all cameras. Yet, surprisingly, they were returned to their owners upon arrival overseas, and the AAF made no further objections to an airman's use of a camera. We even had the Army Photo Service at our disposal. Once a roll of film had been exposed, we got a small drawstring bag from the mail orderly, put in the film and return address slip,

xx

THE WHITE HOUSE
WASHINGTON

TO MEMBERS OF THE UNITED STATES ARMY EXPEDITIONARY
FORCES:

You are a soldier of the United States Army.

You have embarked for distant places where
the war is being fought.

Upon the outcome depends the freedom of your
lives: the freedom of the lives of those you love—
your fellow-citizens—your people.

Never were the enemies of freedom more
tyrannical, more arrogant, more brutal.

Yours is a God-fearing, proud, courageous
people, which, throughout its history, has put its
freedom under God before all other purposes.

We who stay at home have our duties to
perform—duties owed in many parts to you. You will
be supported by the whole force and power of this
Nation. The victory you win will be a victory of all
the people—common to them all.

You bear with you the hope, the confidence,
the gratitude and the prayers of your family, your
fellow-citizens, and your President—

Franklin D Roosevelt

and added the equivalent of fifty or
sixty cents. In about ten days the prints
came back. We could snap almost any-
thing except radar equipment or dead
Americans.

Although deprived of our cameras
while en route, we were given a word of
encouragement in the form of a letter
from our commander in chief.

ACKNOWLEDGMENTS

My special appreciation to Cindy Lee Floyd, without whose encouragement and help this work would never have been accomplished. Thanks also to Patricia G. Flack and Norman V. Waltjen for their careful reviewing of the manuscript.

WITH THE FIFTH ARMY AIR FORCE

A Liberty ship — different from the *General John Pope* but a type of vessel that served the same cargo- and troop-carrying purposes — rests at anchor at Aihoma, Milne Bay, fore and aft painted over for security reasons. During the war U.S. yards turned out more than 2,700 Liberty ships — the largest fleet of a specific type of major vessel ever built. At the end of the twentieth century one of two survivors, the *John W. Brown*, claimed Baltimore as her home port.

TO MILNE BAY, NEW GUINEA

An LCM (landing craft, mechanized) beaches near the location of the Japanese landings of some fourteen months earlier. These boats had twin cylinder Chrysler engines with twin screws, which helped to make them highly maneuverable. They could even be "walked" sideways with application of a sharp rudder and engine direction.

Milne Bay's supply area. This main road was kept in fine condition. In the distance a Jeep heads toward the camera on the left side of the road, British style.

It has been said that if you live long enough, you can expect to undergo "a change in life." We for the most part were not people high up in years. But boarding the troopship USS *General John Pope*, we knew we would all be going through the change of a lifetime. Like ourselves, the *Pope* was fairly untested, having been built just three months earlier, in July 1943 at the Federal Shipbuilding & Drydock Company of Kearny, New Jersey. She was the first of eleven sister troopships built for WWII duties. Six hundred twenty-two feet and seven inches overall in length, and seventy-five and one-half feet of beam, she had a service speed of nineteen knots and could add a knot or two for a short run. Along with everything the ship's crew required for sea-going operations, the *Pope* had facilities for some 5,300 troops. Her maiden voyage had taken her to England and back. Where she would go next we did not know. We left Newport News October 16, 1943.

We were fully loaded; our 33d Fighter Control Squadron—thirty-some officers and 343 enlisted men—was only a small portion of the troops aboard. Each of us received a meal card that we "punched" at chow lines to the tune of but two meals a day—not much sustenance for all the young men and growing boys. The "mind's eye" still pictures some of the voyage—for one thing, its emptiness. We proceeded south and west toward the Panama Canal, all the way without escort vessels. Sometimes—along the East Coast and in the Caribbean—we saw antisubmarine aircraft on patrol. But we were on our own. Once we'd passed through the canal and into the Pacific Ocean, the captain called for frequent gunnery drill, and the racket of deck guns and the larger antiaircraft weapons left a lasting impression. In our case, antisubmarine tactics consisted only of excellent speed and constant zigzagging. No submarine of those days, even surfaced, could approach the

(INSET) We referred to the natives as "Fuzzy-Wuzzies," and at first I thought that we might learn to be as happy in New Guinea as this youngster appeared to be.

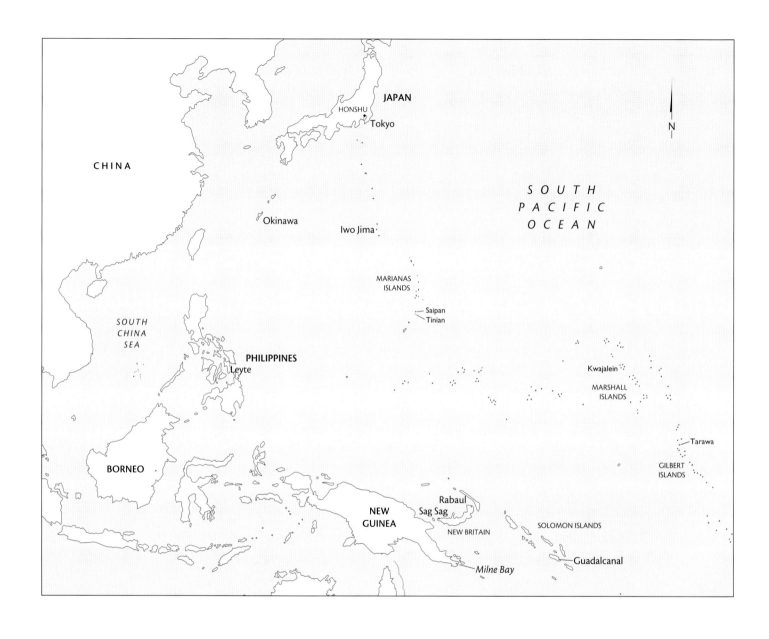

Pope's service speed. I recall but two "sub" alerts on the whole trip.

What many of the troops considered to be the "lowlight" of the journey was the day and a half of full gale our ship encountered. It struck after about twelve to fifteen days of travel in the Pacific. Three out of four of the troops were seasick to one degree or another. To me, the storm was a blessing—no submarines to worry about and, with so many men lying about, more than enough chow. The *Pope* shook, rattled, and rolled, but she held together. A few of the really sick guys said they didn't care if she sunk or not.

When we crossed the Equator the ship's officers, crew, and embarked troops divided dramatically into two groups—those who had made the crossing before (called shellbacks since time unknown) and those miserable creatures who had not (pollywogs). All pollywogs, regardless of rank, found themselves temporarily at the mercy of the shellbacks who, according to custom, devised ceremonies that

included hosing the pollywogs with cold saltwater and making them crawl through muck from the ship's scullery until they had the privilege of kissing the smeared belly of "King Neptune" (a senior petty officer properly garbed for the occasion). Afterwards we new shellbacks received a 21-by-16-inch certificate. Under a drawing of King Neptune himself, the document stated that, because "on the 13th day of October 1943 in latitude ooooo and longitude [blank; our position being a military secret] within the Royal Domain of King Neptune the U.S.S. General John Pope bound south and for Tokyo, 2nd Lt. James P. Gallagher A.C. is worthy to be numbered as one of our Trusty Shellbacks and duly initiated into the Solemn Mysteries of the Ancient Order of the Deep." It was then inscribed with the name Davy Jones, Ruler of the Raging Main, and signed by his servant, George O. Lyn, Captain. Of course I sent it home in a protective cardboard roll and still have it, duly framed, on my wall.

Then there was the pleasure of watching the Exocoetidae. The shell-backs called these maritime creatures "flying fish." We saw them often in the warmer waters of the Pacific Ocean, about a foot to a foot and a half in length. They would leap forward and, with large winglike fins, glide above the water for dozens of feet alongside our ship. They especially liked to frolic in the ship's bow wake. They reminded me of the song from the film *The Road to Mandalay* "where the flying fishes play." Play they did.

We finally received word that our destination was Brisbane, Australia, a port still days away. Simply passing time became a challenge and generally the order of the days. Various card games like gin rummy were popular with some. No gambling was allowed, yet occasionally a quiet crap game turned up. Paperback books and bull sessions had their places. The bo'swain's mate delivered messages loud and clear over the 1MC (ship's PA system), and all announcements were preceded with the classic "Now hear this—now hear this!" The calls lent structure to the long days. Morning, noon, and evening: "Sweepers, man your brooms. Give her a clean sweep down, fore and aft." Later in the evenings, more seriously, "Prepare to darken ship; the smoking lamp is out on all weather decks." Then there were the traditional calls of "Reveille, reveille. All hands heave out and trice up," and "Taps, taps. Lights out."

Our ship finally pulled into Brisbane Harbor, but all we could do was admire the place from a distance. Some "high brass" went ashore to get orders to where we would proceed. After one day we were again on our way. On November 4, 1943, we entered Milne Bay, at the eastern part of New Guinea, and soon debarked. Here Australia and the United States had defeated the Japanese for the first time in the Pacific War. In August 1942 Japanese forces were landed near Lehoa on Milne Bay's north shore. After an intense infantry struggle and ample Allied air support,

Campsite at Milne Bay, taken just a few days after setting up the 33d FCS camp in a recently cleared jungle area. (RIGHT) Same location several weeks later, showing what can be done when everyone pitches in.

Heavy rains cascade water through the 33d FCS camp. Rains came in
torrents at Milne Bay. Note the floor of the tent, made from dunnage
(wooden packing material) from cargo ships, a precious commodity. Long
drainage ditches also helped.

the invasion collapsed, and by the 5th of September the surviving Japanese had evacuated by sea.

We of the 33d Fighter Control Squadron were assigned to the Fifth Air Force, and construction crews cleared a piece of jungle for our new "home" at Aihoma, about a mile east of where the enemy had made its landings. Milne Bay had become a major forward supply base at this time, but even with development it was still an ugly spot to be. The Island of New Guinea has the shape of a bird, so take

Short chow line in the rain. The tin can on the stake at the right of the scene supplied an "ash tray," supposedly keeping cigarette butts from further messing up the place.

Lots of mail was going out, but after a couple of weeks without incoming letters, we held a mock trial and sentenced the mail orderly and his assistant to wear these signs for one day. Stanley F. Zebrowski appears unconcerned about mosquito bites; Charles "Mickey" Masterson is, shall we say, properly garbed.

Charles L. Moody obtains a true GI haircut, while in the tent Irby C. Brown awaits.

A small stream and gravity, combined with scrap lumber and some ingenuity, made for a men's shower. We even managed to attach "shower-heads" to the trough. Joseph Sykora (in coveralls) and 1st Sgt. Edward Krause (center, in towel) did not, at the time, protest the camera's intrusion.

a look at the easternmost "anatomy" of New Guinea and one can imagine the vernacular name for this place we found so miserable. "Acclimate," a word new to most of us, came into general usage. It defined not only adjusting to the tropical heat but becoming accustomed to new environs and various situations. We were getting into the rainy season, when everything quickly either mildewed or rusted. All of the enlisted men had been issued carbines, each commissioned officer a 45-caliber semiautomatic pistol. These weapons needed constant care or rust they would. In just a couple of days one's shoes would begin to turn green. There is no point in belaboring all the inconveniences we were facing, however: even then, we were living in comparative luxury to the lot of the "foot soldier."

Signs of the times. Along a muddy road, a series of signs imitating the manner of stateside Burma Shave advertising read "Take nightly/Rape [crossed out] Reap/the Benefits/of Miss Atabrine 1944." Malaria posed a real danger when the 33d FCS arrived at Milne Bay. The Japanese military typically occupied places where there were natural sources of quinine, the traditional antimalarial medicine, so U.S. forces in the tropics depended on an artificial substance, Atabrine, which the army dispensed in yellow tablets. All of us had to take one a day — "And that's an order!"

GI-produced billboards reminded us of Malaria's threat at every turn — some of them more "military" than others. Others took their inspiration from pinup art. But just a few weeks after I took these pictures, only one of them (predictably, "Which Is Hotter?") remained. It seems a chaplain had something to say about the genre's vulgarity. MCU stood for Medical Corp Unit; the signature on the mosquito-net billboard was that of Cyril Jones.

For some reason the Australians and the British tagged the venerable Douglas C-47 the *Dakota*, one of them here sitting at an airstrip near Gili Gili at Milne Bay. The AAF's approved name for the C-47 was *Skytrain*, a name I never heard used. We always simply said *C-47*.

At the same strip, a Bristol Beaufort taxis down the runway after a reconnaissance mission. Some Beauforts were built in Australia under license from the British company.

Remains of a Japanese landing barge destroyed during the enemy attempt to occupy Milne Bay. Much live ammunition remained in the surrounding waters.

Japanese landing barges in the Gili Gili area of Milne Bay, November 1943. We usually saw them only in shambles from bombings and strafings; the Aussies captured these two, still intact, during the Japanese invasion attempt and pressed them into service against their original owners. In the background, salvage parties work on an Australian freighter that capsized after a Japanese air raid in April.

ORO BAY / DOBODURA, NEW GUINEA

The 33d left Milne Bay in late November 1943, heading west to Oro Bay, a forward staging area where we were to receive full equipment for future operations. We shipped aboard a Dutch merchantman, the *Tjisadane*, which was crewed by mostly Javanese sailors. Built in Amsterdam in 1931, she was by no means a pleasure liner, but she carried, and we appreciated, her comparatively heavy armament. The uneventful trip took only two days. We disembarked in what were nicknamed *Ducks*, basically floating two-and-one-half-ton trucks.

Compared to the conditions at Milne Bay, Oro was delightful. Instead of setting up in thick and ugly jungles, we made camp on a coastal plain with lots of kunai grass. The level ground readily absorbed rains instead of turning into a quagmire—a welcome blessing. Dunnage was rather scarce here, but it was not as necessary as at Milne. A few of the fellows made small platforms for their cots. Worldly goods were hung on tent posts or set on boxes or small boards. We had a waterfront property with a small beach area, so we built a pier and went swimming when off duty. Oro Bay even had a place of worship, Palm Beach Chapel. It served different faiths and was quite a contraption.

Oro Bay lay about seven or eight miles southeast of Buna and the major U.S. air base at Dobodura, or Dobo. Photographically speaking, Dobo was easily the main attraction. In the single year it had been in operation, it had developed into a great air base complex. My friend Joe Sykora and I had to see what was going on at Dobo firsthand, so we rode our thumbs a couple of times to make "inspection" trips. We got to see plenty, as there were lots of P-39s, P-40s (some of which were Aussie Kittyhawks), P-38s, A-20s, a couple of P-70s, plus plenty of B-24s, B-25s, and C-47s. All had one thing in common in that they wore camouflage paints. Some of these aircraft were tired and dusty looking, as a result of many months in a tropical environment.

There was an exception—a squadron of Glenn L. Martin–made B-26s. Since we shared the same hometown, I especially wanted to get a real good look at them. Joe and I managed to chat with some of the B-26 ground crew members. The planes belonged to the 19th Bombardment Squadron, 22d Bomber Group (composed of the 19th and three other squadrons, the 2d, the 33d, and the 408th).

The 22d had gone into action during the early days of the war, flying the "hot" sixty-five-foot-wingspan B-26. In March and April 1942, some four dozen of this group arrived at Archerfield, an air base near Brisbane, Australia. They were quickly moved up north to a field in the Townsville area. On April 5 some of these bombers took off for what was to be the B-26's first combat mission of the war. The target was Rabaul, in New Britain, which the Japanese were building into the hub of their activities in the South Pacific. From Townsville the 26s flew hundreds of miles across the Coral Sea to Port Moresby, in New Guinea, for refueling at Seven Mile Strip, a rough and barely usable advanced base. After topping off the tanks, they flew another 500 miles to reach Rabaul. The last mission of this series was flown on May 24, 1942.

We made our own amenities. Contemplating our next move to bigger things while enjoying the surf are (left to right) Jim Lynch, Joe Harlan, and Don Nickell. Tom McCraley (INSET) poses in front of a shared tent; this row is typical of the whole outfit's living area. (ABOVE) Ray Scheid does his laundry beside our latest homemade shower, a 55-gallon oil drum hoisted up with commandeered lumber.

In July 1943, flying out of Dobodura, the all-B-26 19th BS became the first unit of the 22d BG to return to action and the first in the Southwest Pacific Area (SWPA) to add a new element to winged warfare—the removal of all camouflage paint on combat duty. American attacks on Rabaul resumed that fall, when the Lae-Salamaua areas, especially airfields and supply dumps, received much attention from the Marauders of the 22d BG. After about ten months of wear and tear, the 22d was withdrawn from combat. The Fifth Air Force received no more B-26 replacements, and the aircraft type moved to the European theater. Many of the Pacific B-26s' later combat missions were directed at western New Britain, softening up the place for the Cape Gloucester show. Targets were barge hideouts, shipping lanes, supply areas, antiaircraft positions, airfields, and defense installations.

Officially named the Marauder, the early B-26—technically challenging to pilots—earned other names, among

Glenn L. Martin advertisement, Marauders in New Guinea.

Army Air Force cameras capture some of the action during a raid on the Japanese airfield at Rapopo, Rabaul.

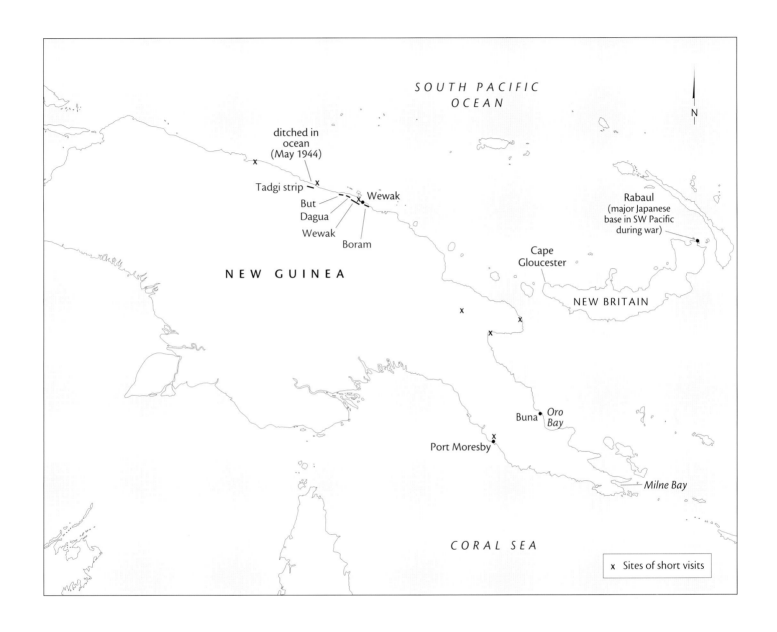

SOUTH PACIFIC
OCEAN

ditched in
ocean
(May 1944)

Tadgi strip

But

Dagua

Wewak

Boram

Wewak

NEW GUINEA

Rabaul
(major Japanese
base in SW Pacific
during war)

Cape
Gloucester

NEW BRITAIN

Buna
Oro
Bay

Port Moresby

Milne Bay

CORAL SEA

N

x   Sites of short visits

Joe Sykora takes an admiring look at a Marauder at Dobo.

them the *Flying Prostitute* (no visible means of support), the *Widow Maker,* the *Flying Cigar,* and the *Baltimore Whore.* Nonetheless pleased to be flying so distinctive an aircraft, the men of the 19th BS adopted the name *Silver Fleet* and devised a distinctive insignia rudder display. The best press for the outfit came by way of Radio Tokyo, which beamed slanted news and propaganda broadcasts in English to the South Pacific. Tokyo Rose delivered the Silver Fleet some nasty threats; the Marauder men noted them proudly. In January 1944, at Dobo, I had a picture of myself taken standing beside the *Pistol Packin' Mama* and sent a print to my brother, who at the time was working at the Martin plant in Baltimore. A crewman told me that this B-26 was being readied for final flight to Australia to meet the rest of the Silver Fleet. She was the last Marauder we saw. (But she was not the last silver aircraft; by mid-1944, some new planes in natural metal finish appeared, and, by the end of the year, there were a good number of unpainted aircraft of various types in combat.)

Through the years, I have kept in contact with one of the great Pacific aces, Robert M. DeHaven of the 7th Fighter Squadron, 49th Fighter Group. In one of his letters, referring to the B-26s, he recalls: "We called them the last of the Silver Fleet in as much as they were to be the last Marauders to serve in the SWPA and were flying sans camouflage. I flew several missions escorting them on strikes to Salamaua and Lae in mid-1943. In all honesty escorting meant rendezvousing with

This B-25 D of the 498th BS, cockpit window cloaked to the sun, vividly displays its falcon insignia and conquests. The name *Near Miss* was painted below the cockpit on the starboard side. The sign on the armament gives fair warning—"Guns Clear."

A B-25 Mitchell medium bomber standing in dispersal at Dobodura.

them over the target during their strikes and little more. They were much faster than our P-40s so we had to reach the target before them and then on the way home watch them fly off and leave us. They were such beautiful machines."

During the heyday of the Silver Fleet, the other squadrons of the 22d BG flew the North American B-25, named the *Mitchell* for the champion of air power between the world wars, General Billy Mitchell. Not as sturdy or as fast as the Marauder, and carrying a lighter bomb load, the Mitchell nevertheless had better range and could operate off of shorter strips—priority factors in the SWPA. The B-25 started with the Fifth Air Force as a medium bomber that was only lightly armed and was supposed to function at so-called medium altitudes. A few B-25s were equipped with a hand-loaded 75-millimeter cannon. This variation had only limited success. It was as a strafer that the Mitchell excelled, and later in the war some were armed with eight 50-caliber machine guns in the nose, plus a pair of 50s mounted on each side —all firing forward. The top turret's guns could be aimed in the same direction.

The flat sides of the B-25 invited works of "art," the source of inspiration rarely straying far from the male libido. Below are *Our Gal II*, a B-25 of the 33d BS, and *Bashful D*, a B-25 of the 49th BS.

A B-24 "Lib" moves off its hardstand and kicks up a local dust storm at Dobo.

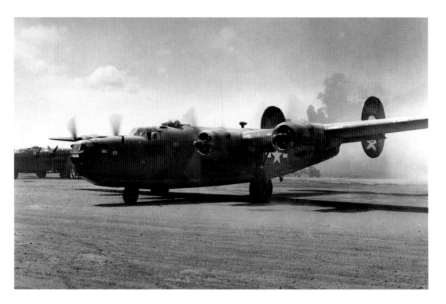

The 22d BG entered combat as a medium bombardment outfit, but in the early weeks of 1944 the army converted it to a heavy bombing group. Its B-25s went to other SWPA units. Combat-ready B-17 Flying Fortresses had become almost nonexistent. B-24 Liberators arrived, and the 22d adopted the name *Red Raiders*.

The P-38 Lockheed Lightning started arriving on the SWPA combat scene in small numbers very late in 1942 and during the first few months of 1943. As their numbers increased, so did the woe of the Japanese flyers. Designed as an interceptor, the 38 made the enemy pay dearly in plane losses. The much-vaunted Japanese Zero, which for a time had been the hunter, became the hunted, especially when the Japanese attempted daylight air raids. The Lightning also proved its worth as an escort fighter. At Dobodura in December 1942, I took some pictures of the 475th Fighter Group, the only fighter group activated in the SWPA during World War II. The group was built around

A beautiful sky sets the scene for a flight of five B-24s over Oro Bay returning from a mission.

Ground crews tend to P-38s in dispersal.

Lightning No. 154 makes a high-speed approach at Dobodura strip. (INSET) A formation of P-38s flies overhead at Dobo in a large V formation. They belonged to the 432d Fighter Squadron, 475th FG.

Joe Sykora poses with a group of Aussies and natives, all eager to get into the picture.

men who were, for the most part, veterans of the Pacific air war, and from start to finish the unit flew only P-38s in combat. At war's end it stood second in air victories among AAF fighter groups of the Pacific war, trailing only the famous 49th Fighter Group. P-38 pilots considered their planes the Cadillac of America's fighters.

After close to a year of brutal fighting, Buna—a short distance to the northwest of Oro—developed by late 1943 into an advanced staging base for the Aussies. Joe Sykora and I visited

This little boy came with his own drum.

Native men and boys played a game that reminded me of the boardwalk at Ocean City — pitching balls, actually coconuts, and trying to knock over targets that had faces painted on them.

Buna twice, the first time in mid-December. Joe wanted me to photograph him with a couple of natives, which I was about to do when a group of Aussies and more natives insisted on getting in the act — thus the spontaneous gathering of musicians, dancers, and people happy to have their portraits taken for (my) posterity.

Seldom did any of us see, much less

Japanese War Cemetery, Buna.

Remains of a Japanese antiaircraft gun.

photograph, a Japanese military cemetery in a forward area. I came upon this one in December at Buna. Only a few of its grave markers carried positive identification; most referred to unidentified soldiers. Those on our side presumably had made the burials, a rare display of respect for the then-hated enemy.

CAPE GLOUCESTER, NEW BRITAIN

By January 1944 the 33d Fighter Control Squadron at Oro Bay had made itself ready for full operations. We then moved on to Cape Gloucester, New Britain Island, a mostly inhospitable piece of real estate some three hundred miles long, averaging forty to fifty miles across. The marines had made their assault on Cape Gloucester the day after Christmas in 1943 and, after heavy fighting, had secured the beachhead, the immediate surrounding area, and the airfield. Further operations at the cape were meant to secure the eastern flank of MacArthur's campaigns on New Guinea, as well as to assist in the reduction and isolation of Rabaul, which—at a distance of about three hundred miles—remained a great military complex. Too costly an enemy base to attack with a landing force, it was militarily isolated by the spring of 1944, a nuisance to be kept neutralized. To cover the 265 nautical miles from Oro Bay to the cape, the 33d boarded an LST (or landing ship, tank—often referred to as "long, slow target") in a small convoy. Our unit beached on February 1 after a small advanced echelon had moved there days before.

We of the 33d had the job of establishing a communication center for what was known as a fighter sector, coordinating Air Force operations with Signal Corps radar stations linked to antiaircraft artillery. Each of these sectors required a center that processed all operational data: radio reports, air movements, interceptions, antiaircraft units, homing and intelligence knowledge. For our purposes, a diesel-powered electric generator—along with a shed to protect it—was fully as important as food, transportation,

Transmitter shack, Cape Gloucester, and a view inside the shack, with all its radios and communications equipment.

shelter, and medical assistance. At every new site, we also had to build an operations center for the air controllers and install a radio transmitter center with all its equipment. We called the advance base operation center "the shack." Controllers sat in the catbird seats overlooking the plotting board. The radio call sign for the Cape Gloucester Sector was EMBAY.

During our first month at the cape,

in February 1944, we faced few daytime enemy sorties (we called them sneak raiders) but about three dozen separate night air raids. These attacks consisted of one to eight enemy airplanes, or simply bandits, usually coming from Rabaul, sometimes from one of the smaller Japanese strips within range, those to the south being closest to us. Strips to the northwest were Boram, Wewak, Dagua, But, and Tadgi—all of

The sector also relied on this HF/DF (High Frequency, Direction Finding) tower. The operator used the tower, with its fully rotating base, to guide planes onto the nearby airfield. The sides were removable.

(LEFT) Bill Boyle operates the tower, its sides removed. (CENTER) Herschel Taylor, the outfit's best man for fixing radio equipment and keeping the 33d on the air, at work on radio equipment. (RIGHT) We set up the 33d FCS switchboard about five feet below grade, within a tent. This trenched area was chosen with safety in mind for the operator and equipment. Note the readily available helmet.

Searchlight and antiaircraft fire at night.

which were on the New Guinea coast and provided targets for our own daylight attacks. In one of the two photos I snapped while having nothing more pressing to do, time exposure captured marine antiaircraft fire while a searchlight spotted a Japanese raider—a twin-engine bomber that soon came down, finished off. Most of the time the fighter sector people on duty knew of an incoming raid well in advance of it. At the time, we credited our radar and the coast watchers in the hills; after the war we learned that the United States had broken the Japanese military code and thus had another source of advance warnings. We had, as it were, been "reading their mail for a long time."

As the strength of the Fifth Air Force increased, the Japanese navy pulled its combat craft and transport ships from around Cape Gloucester and, working out of Rabaul, resorted instead to

U.S. aerial reconnaissance photo of Japanese base
at Lukunai, near Rabaul.

U.S. aircraft hit Rabaul often and hard in late 1943 and early 1944.
Bombing-run photos of Fifth Army Air Force attacks on the Japanese airfield at Dagua, mostly the work of treetop-flying B-25s.

A small Japanese armored patrol craft met its end at Sag Sag.

Allied air attacks made a shambles of the enemy's barge hideout at Borgan Bay, Cape Gloucester.

landing barges to move troops and supplies. Moving in darkness, they would pull into barge hideouts at daybreak. Constant air reconnaissance soon located many of the ports, and attacks followed. Their losses were severe. At the cape, the marines captured a raft of military weapons, especially anti-aircraft guns. Some of these were fixed at a given site; others were mobile for quick change of location. When we first approached our landing spot we saw two or three lighters loaded with some Japanese aircraft in various stages of damage. I later learned that the marines had found an operational Tony

Captured Japanese AA guns, one a light, rapid-firing type.

fighter hidden in the woods, a great prize for intelligence study.

For much of early 1944, living conditions at the cape recalled the well-known song "I Never Promised You a Rose Garden." The U.S. move into Cape Gloucester took place during the northwest monsoon season, mid-December through March. In terms of weather, New Britain during this season was one of the worst spots to be in during the war. The season brought frequent middle-of-the-night thunderstorms. The worst, in February 1944, produced lightning bolts for three hours and killed four men. A few other

By March 1944 American forces had thoroughly secured the Cape Gloucester area. This photo of the marine cemetery there, which I took as a reminder of the terrible cost of reclaiming territory from the Japanese military, has the look of a Civil War daguerreotype because I snapped it while holding the camera lens to the eyepiece of a mounted eight-power pair of binoculars that belonged to a nearby marine anti-aircraft unit.

Driving his Jeep outside our area, Wing Huey, a Chinese-American with the 33d, was briefly captured by some marines. He received a military escort (for his own safety) back to the 33d area with orders to stay within the campsite.

insects, including disease-carrying mosquitos, ticks, and oversized spiders. Centipedes were on hand, plus an incredible supply of scorpions. Large rats moved about, oblivious to the humans. Officers had a slight advantage in that their quarters were less crowded than the enlisted men's. All tents had their foxholes for air raid protection. Our dearest luxury was a fast, clear-running stream around our campsite, which was in constant use. By April, living conditions had greatly improved. Wires had been strung and each tent had an electric lightbulb. Three movies a day were shown in a makeshift theater. We had a mess hall and a volleyball court. All in all, things got better. Even the airfield got its improvements.

Inspired by aircraft nose art and the arrival of spring, Stanley Chicoski decided to paint *Millie* on our Tech Supply Jeep. I of course approved and even posed in the tastefully decorated vehicle. In the next panel of this comic strip, Ken Woodford was driving me in

servicemen (no one in the 33d) were actually killed by falling trees. The soil was thoroughly saturated with volcanic ash, and a continually smoking volcano, Mount Langla, lay just beyond Mount Talawa.

Cape Gloucester was infested with

Comparative view of a Cape Gloucester bug and a pack of Lucky Strikes.

Two views of the enlisted men's area at the cape. Mt. Talawa, rising 6,600 feet, stands in the background at right.

Taking the waters at Cape Gloucester and shaving at the officer's vanity, double bowl (helmets) and a water supply at hand.

First mail call at Cape Gloucester. Even though dampness affected this negative, the picture still captures the flavor of the occasion. As a security measure, the army made sure that assigned APO (Army Post Office) numbers left no clue as to location. Cape Gloucester's number was 320. Oro Bay was APO 503 unit one, Milne Bay APO 928.

Our makeshift theater gave us a place to see movies at night and, during the day, at "required attendance" sessions, to absorb lectures on health and safety from Doc Lipchutz. We tried to listen carefully. Most every unit had its "entertainer," and the 33d had two, Bob Mulligan and George Beam. Here George acknowledges the applause of assembled fans on the volleyball court.

As commanding officer of the 33d, Maj. Howard E. Smith guided us from Philadelphia to the forward area of operations at the cape, whereupon he left us for a higher level of responsibility within the Fifth AAF. Capt. Charles P. Mead replaced him.

The Tech Supply group worked out of the settlement on the left of the Jeep road, which cut through tough kunai grass. The group assembles here for a portrait, leaving legible a GI-humor sign that reads, "We ain't got it. We can't get it." Standing, left to right, are Hurschel Thomas, Stanley Watkins, and Lt. Don Nickell. Front, left to right, are Vernel "Tex" Venable, Herschel Taylor, Ken Woodford, and Ed Nevill. When, in April 1944, Nickell received orders for another post within the 33d, I replaced him as Tech Supply officer.

Stanley
Chicoski
painting
Millie.

The marine general missed my civilian footwear.

Millie when a marine Jeep with a big white star on its front passed us from the opposite direction. I saluted smartly. About a hundred yards to the rear, the general's driver turned about, chased us down, and pulled us over. I got out and stood at attention. After I identified myself proudly as belonging to the Army Air Force's 33d Fighter Control Squadron, the general gave me holy hell for desecrating an army Jeep and mistreating government property. He gave me a direct order to return *Millie Ampere* to strict GI format. Deeply wounded in spirit and flushed with interservice rivalry, I had to wonder what would happen if he ever got around an army field and had a good look at the personalized fuselages.

Adding to my "distinguished service," I took my first airplane trip in May. Tech Supply needed radio tubes and parts, so we prepared a requisition sheet, and orders were cut sending me to a supply depot at Nadzab, on New Guinea. That morning I went to the Gloucester strip and waited for a courier plane. While I was there an Aussie Bristol Beaufort landed, and I went over to where it was parked. The pilot, Flight Officer C. Macnaughton, told me that the plane was on a courier mission to Aitape, with Nadzab its base upon completion of the trip. Upon seeing my orders, he told me to "hop aboard." That I did, and shortly we were on our way.

After a lengthy flight we arrived over Aitape and approached its Tadgi strip (now secured from the Japanese), prepared to land. A red flare and a red light signal from the control tower sent us away. Macnaughton gave the plane

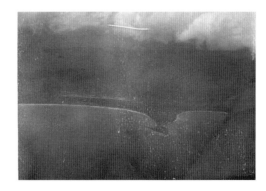

Water-damaged aerial view of Japanese airfield, Boram Strip.

full power and we climbed out to sea to get back into a landing pattern. Just a few miles from land, things went awry—the starboard engine caught fire, and moments later the port engine sputtered to a stop. The pilot leveled the plane just before we hit the water; we bounced once, then stopped sharply. In seconds, the four Aussies and I escaped the wrecked plane. The pilot quickly released the rubber life raft from the port wing. Thank God it inflated, for in another minute Beaufort No. 572 sank. We were in the raft for less than an hour before a small boat came out to take us to shore. My travel bag with its contents went down with the plane; my camera, hanging over my shoulder, was ruined by the saltwater swim. Only one negative, showing the recently neutralized Boram Strip at Wewak, somewhat survived.

The day following the crash-landing we all made it back east in a C-47, and, after being stranded for a week at Nadzab, I finally got a VIP flight back to Gloucester, riding in the rear cockpit of a P-70 Havoc. The pilot had a grand time with his plane, and so did I. When I got "home" there was mail for me, including six rolls of 120-millimeter film that my folks had rounded up. I made a deal with Roy Pipino, who had a nice camera but no film, and I was back in business. One of the most unusual planes I saw at the cape was the Supermarine Walrus, which made a refueling and minor maintenance stop in June 1944. It was named *Rescuer's Angel* and carried a lovely image of a mermaid. On the port side there were painted rows of fourteen stretchers, along with six of what were probably life rafts.

In July I received a piece of paper to put with my shellback certificate. Having survived the ditching of an aircraft at sea, I became a proud member of the Goldfish Club, American Division. I later learned that the group had originated with a British emergency dinghy manufacturer who wished to reward users of his product—and call RAF attention to it. The British club conferred life membership only on

Supermarine Walrus, parked near a C-47.

Dear Member:

We are pleased to welcome you as a member of the GOLDFISH
CLUB.

As you probably know, this exclusive organization is composed
of airmen all over the world who, like yourself, have survived a water landing.

Your insignia and membership card are enclosed. We also
enclose a booklet on the Club which will be of special interest to you as a member.

We look forward to meeting you personally if, at any time, you
find it convenient to visit Chicago.

We don't have to tell you that you really _earned_ this membership; you can well be proud of it.

Best wishes,

THE GOLDFISH CLUB

Max Karant

MaxKarant:mhs   American Secretary

Please keep us informed of any changes in your home address.

A troop-carrying C-47, June 1944, and (BELOW) a C-47 *Speedy Steede*.

airmen who had saved their lives in an inflatable dinghy, offering something less to the rest. But in true democratic fashion, the American branch welcomed victims regardless of whether they had been saved by dinghies, life jackets, or floating wreckage.

By June 1944, traffic at Cape Gloucester slacked off. The cape was becoming a backwater. At the end of May, the marines left for regrouping, GIs of the 40th Division taking their

Navy Hellcats visit Cape Gloucester.

An Army AF P-38.

place. Courier planes still passed through Gloucester, but airfield traffic slowed to the proverbial crawl. Since March, virtually all of Rabaul's operational aircraft had flown to the island of Truk, in the central Caroline Islands. Intelligence reported the fact to Gloucester, and the P-40s based there left. The arrival of U.S. combat planes became an event. In June a pair of navy F-6F Hellcats made a refueling stop at

Two Boomerangs buzz by the Gloucester strip.

Boomerangs in a protective revetment.

A Vultee Vengeance as an Aussie A-35. The AAF used a few of these craft, unsuccessfully, during the early days of the war in New Guinea. This plane, its front circled by vapor trails from the spinning prop, served as a courier. A storm approaches from the mountains.

the cape. I did not know, and still cannot imagine, what navy fighters were doing there. They did make an attractive subject for some camera work, however, as did a P-38, which I shot with the rugged terrain of this part of New Britain in the background, and Australian Boomerangs, which now provided the cape its fighter protection.

In late June 1944, as the battle for Normandy raged in Europe, the vari-ous Melanesian tribes in the Cape Gloucester region held a conference and called for a gathering to celebrate the driving out of the Japanese forces. Since the 33d FCS had been in Gloucester for what seemed like a long time, I took it upon myself to act as an unofficial representative. I, too, was glad that the Japanese had left this place. Jim Lynch went with me and took a shot of me parading.

A native shrouded in jungle growth leads a celebration while a group of tribesmen gather to celebrate.

Jim Lynch with Cape Gloucester native.

A light surf washes in from Dampier Strait, June 1944; Sakar Island lies in the distance. Peaceful and secure, but not quite a tropical paradise. (INSET) A tentative celebration, but wholly enjoyable.

LCMs were a sine qua non for the success of Middelburg Island as a viable air base. After being grounded on Middelburg's shore by a stiff breeze, this LCM requires the help of a bulldozer to refloat the craft and complete its assignment. In the background is the shoreline of the Sansapor mainland.

SANSAPOR AND MIDDELBURG, NEW GUINEA

Time had come to pack up and move things out of Cape Gloucester. There was still a big war going on, but it was taking place many miles north and west of us. Also by that time—thanks to the caring attention of our outfit's supply sergeant, Jim Haley—the clothing of mine that had been lost in the Beaufort's ditching was now fully replaced. One more thing—my parents had mailed me an old camera from home that had been stored away in the attic. It was not a very good one, an old folding No.1 Pocket Kodak. Using 120-millimeter film, it had a 6:3 lens and two shutter speeds (1/25 and 1/50 of a second). Promotion to first lieutenant meant far less to me than having my own working camera.

Everyone and all equipment embarked aboard a Liberty ship at Borgen Bay for the move. We went westerly in a small convoy escorted by a couple of patrol craft. Around the middle of July, we anchored in Maffin Bay, off Arara. Arara was located on the mainland just west of Wadke Island. Remarkably, what was formerly a Japanese staging area had become an important base for U.S. forces. I got the dubious honor of being put in charge of unloading the ship. It was quite an experience—especially working at night with all the lights on in a hostile area. Tons of equipment were hauled ashore. We immediately established a temporary campsite. After just a few days' stopover there, the men and equipment next boarded LSTs and headed west for Sansapor, where we landed on July 30, 1944. Sansapor lay at the northwesternmost point of Dutch New Guinea (now Indonesia), with two small islands nearby—Amsterdam, three miles off

Two of the 33d's controllers on duty at Middelburg. In the white shirt is Lt. Stu Johnson on the land line while Lt. Ray Scheid is on the air (all controllers were officers). This Fighter Sector employed the radio call sign AUTO.

the coast (about one mile long by half a mile wide), and Middelburg, about a mile east of Amsterdam (a mile long by five-eighths of a mile wide). Middelburg was called, with proper respect, the Reef. The navy used the water off Amsterdam to station a large seaplane tender, mothering two or three PBMs (Martin patrol bombers, called Mariners), whose range and versatility were instrumental.

After beaching, we moved to an assigned section of the wretched jungle where we prepared to set up another fighter sector center. Work began on two airfields—a fighter strip on Middelburg and a bomber base on the mainland. We were, for the time being, the most advanced Allied base in the Southwest Pacific theater—the farthest outpost on MacArthur's road to the Philippines. The Allies had leap-frogged again, this time over the defensive hump at Manokwari, isolating thousands of Japanese troops there. Upon completion of the two new strips, the Allies had air bases established from Milne Bay along the entire coast of New Guinea.

Somebody up the chain of command decided to establish the fighter sector

Plotting board overlook.

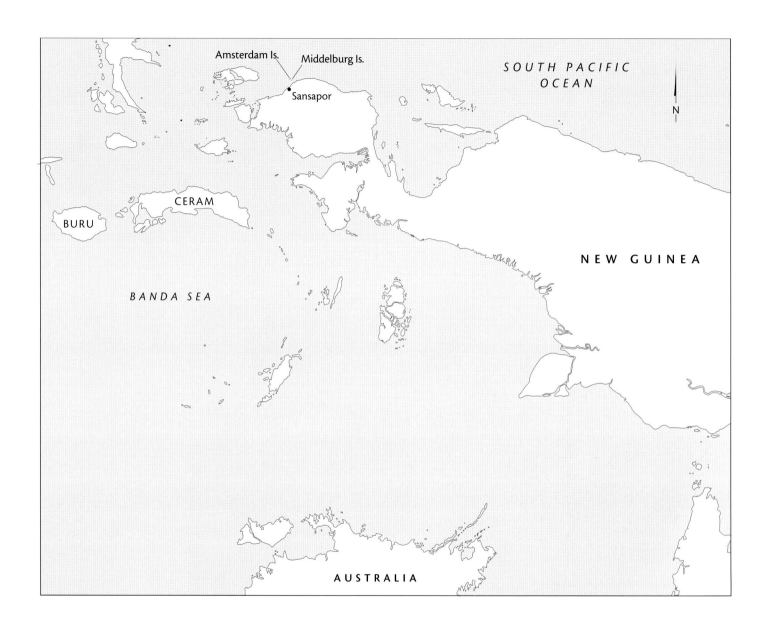

center on the Reef rather than the mainland at Sansapor, the main reason being that, after a rather narrow coastal plain area, the hills and mountains took over. The offshore site gave radar a better sweep of the sky for all aircraft. Meantime, remarkably, the Japanese never hit us with daylight air raids. There were many enemy airdromes in range of our area, many even quite nearby. There were strips at Manokwari, Ransiki, Moemi, Sawate, Sagan, Otawari, Utarom, Babo, Samate, and Jefman. Allied bombers and fighters did such yeoman work in beating up these bases that we virtually eliminated them as offensive threats.

By mid-August construction units had the strip at Middelburg ready for full operations, and a group of P-38s of the Thirteenth Air Force made this their base. A pair of PBYs (amphibious patrol bombers made by Consolidated and known as Catalinas) based there, too. At about the same time, a bomber strip on the mainland became home for a B-25 group.

A closer view of targets on our plotting board, the easiest and simplest way to track the whereabouts of our planes—and known bandits.

Tracers pouring over our 33d campsite, aimed at low-flying attackers.

to the high seas. Why be the proverbial sitting duck during air attacks? The enemy planes sometimes came from Namlea, on Boeroe, or from a Boela airdrome on Ceram. Most staged at Jefman, west of Sorong. They typically came armed with daisy cutter bombs, which had rods at the head and, upon contact with the ground, would spray deadly shrapnel over a wide area.

These Japanese forays had mixed results. One four-plane strike suc-

The time now arrived for some Japanese night work in the area. Sansapor strip received a couple of twin-engine bomber attacks; we on the Reef endured a series of eight to ten night raids by low-flying, single-engine attackers, usually Sonias flying in three to five individual sorties. Several times our controllers had advance warnings of impending attacks. Given enough time (or as a simple precaution as dusk approached), the skipper of the PBM tender would weigh anchor and head out

Damage done to the radio equipment and radio shack.

Middelburg's control tower — a typical GI control tower at the strip. The tower's operators took refuge as necessary in the bomb shelter at the right. It stood above grade, not dug into the ground, because the hard, concrete-like coral precluded the digging of a typical shelter.

ceeded in destroying a half-dozen P-38s and damaging others while also rupturing the fuel line on the jetty, setting off a large fire. Radio Tokyo reported in perfect English that the Imperial Wild Eagles had made a mess of the Middelburg area, offering much detail. The enemy did not know that the attack that night knocked the 33d FCS off the air for ten hours.

Stationed on a small coral island with a barely basic camera, one would wisely choose photographic subjects with care. Fortunately, as a forward field, the Reef provided a landing place for various aircraft types not generally seen at AAF bases. The planes joined us for refueling and minor maintenance stopovers.

By early fall, living conditions on

Our tent at Middelburg.

A two-tent, shared deluxe bomb shelter—more than a foxhole. From left to right: Jim Lynch, Fletcher Hornbaker, Ray Scheid, me, and John Robey.

the Reef were bordering on comfortable. Movies were shown a couple of nights a week, the food situation had improved, and night raids had ceased. Our tent quarters were upgraded nicely. As usual, however, the war proved unpredictable. In October orders came down from headquarters, 86th Fighter Wing, reassigning me to the 49th Fighter Group, APO 920, by military aircraft. APO 920 was at Biak, a spot on the map about 240 miles to the east. The honor of being assigned to the reputable 49th somewhat eased the pain of leaving old friends of the 33d.

The war had left New Guinea and New Britain behind. We might think

A B-24 as seen from under the wing of another B-24. In late August 1944, a couple of the 90th Bomber Group's B-24s made a refueling stop at Middelburg. They were shiny new Liberators that called for a couple of photos. The 90th BG, with its four squadrons (319, 320, 321, and 400) and distinguished service record, was one of the most famous bomber groups of the Pacific war. The group's white skull and cross-bombs insignia was never to be forgotten. It was placed on the tails of all the 90th planes, and different background colors identified the various squadrons. The group was aptly named the Jolly Rogers.

A B-24 of the 20th Combat Mapping Squadron.

The British-built
Bristol Beaufighter
could be a deadly
attacker.

An Aussie Mosquito being refueled, then
taking off at Middelburg. A rare bird in the
SWPA, the British-built de Havilland Mosquito
served the Australians as a photo-reconnais-
sance plane. The Mosquito carried no
armament, relying on its great speed to get to
its target and back. It simply outran any
Japanese who might try to intercept. I have
never seen a photo elsewhere or heard tell of
this plane serving in the Pacific war against
Japan.

that history itself had moved on; as important as Middelburg Island was to the Allied advance, it does not even show as a flyspeck on a three-by-four-foot map of Southeast Asia printed in 1995. The Dutch quit the western end of the island in 1963; twelve years later the Australians granted the people of the eastern side complete independence as Papua New Guinea. Name changes since then have been commonplace (Hollandia now goes by Jayapura). But I will never forget the exotic names of places (besides sites of the 33d's service) where I went for radio supplies, stopped for refueling, passed through, visited, or was temporarily stranded: Gili Gili, Cape Sudest, Dobodura, Buna, Soputa, Sananada, Horando, Finschhafen, Lae, Nadzab, Tsili Tsili, Dumpu, Saidor, Aitape, Borgen Bay, Sag Sag, Los Negros, Port Moresby, Hollandia, Sarmi, Noemfoor, Biak, Anguar. This list is in no order.

A B-25 at Middelburg, stopped over for reloading and refueling.

An AAF A-24 Douglas Dauntless, another plane rarely seen, stops at and takes off from Middelburg in September 1944. The Navy version, the SBD, earned lasting fame for sinking four Japanese carriers during the Battle of Midway, changing the tide of the Pacific war. A few A-24s went into combat in New Guinea in late 1942, but losses were so great that what planes remained were pulled from the battles. The army used this surviving A-24 as a VIP transporter.

A PBY Catalina in a true tropical setting. One can understand why sunglasses were quite a necessity, Middelburg Island was only about twenty-five miles south of the Equator.

A rare view of a sparkling NMF (natural metal finish) P-40N that belonged to the 49th FG, photographed in September 1944 during a stopover at Middelburg. While the 49th FG's 9th Squadron had been a P-38 outfit for well over a year, its 7th and 8th Squadrons were still using P-40s (though receiving P-38s). This particular craft had 8th Squadron colors, with the prop spinner and tail tip in deep yellow and black finish. Nevertheless, it was probably a shared plane with the 7th.

Convoy as seen from lead LST, the ship's wake clearly visible in the calm Pacific, on or about October 20. The scene at dusk, LSTs in convoy headed to the Philippines.

TO LEYTE, WITH THE 49TH FIGHTER GROUP

My orders to leave Middelburg were clear, and two days later I jumped aboard an LST carrying the water echelon of the 9th Fighter Squadron along with 49th Fighter Group Headquarters people. From Biak, we sailed in a small convoy to Hollandia to join a large convoy for the invasion of the Philippines. We all received a thirty-four-page booklet—printed on pulp paper—entitled "To the Philippines." Though our destination was no secret, the exact time and place of our landing was not generally known by the GIs. We were the lead ship of Reinforcement Group 2, the last of the so-called

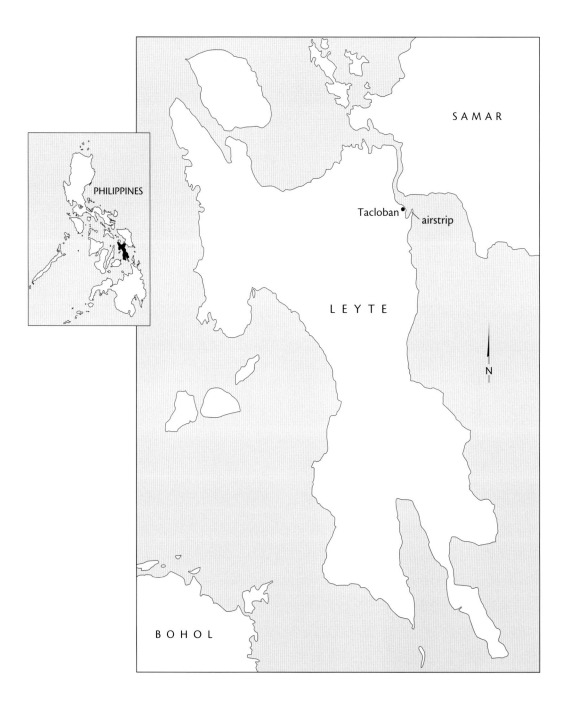

assault force, scheduled to arrive at Leyte the morning of October 24, 1944, "A day" plus four. MacArthur had chosen the term *A day* for the assault, foregoing the commonly used *D day*; for the general, this campaign fulfilled the promise he had made in his famous quote, "I shall return." Note that he never used the word *we*.

Our convoy—blessed with near-perfect weather, zigzagging all the way —consisted of thirty-three LSTs, twenty-four Liberty ships, nine service-force vessels, and one oiler. Four destroyers and two frigates escorted us. At dusk we heard the familiar call for a blackout: "The smoking lamp is out on all weather decks." The convoy commodore happened to be aboard our LST, and he was a gracious skipper. Having some meals and socializing with him was a great experience. He gave me an open invitation to visit the wheelhouse and chart room. One day during the voyage, under his supervision, I took the helm—and led the convoy—for a good half hour. Having

Filipinos greet us in a small outrigger boat.

left Leyte Gulf, our convoy did not receive, nor did we expect, a royal welcome as we sailed to San Pedro Bay. Our LST, as point vessel, did enjoy the reception the first Filipinos gave us. We heard for the first time the rapturous call, "Victoreee!" The GIs at the LST's rail were fascinated at this spontaneous welcome we Americans were getting.

The cheery welcome we received was short-lived. I heard on the radio in

Our LST lays a smoke screen.

fighter bomber headed for Samar at a good 350-mile-per-hour clip, racing to get out of range of the navy's heavy antiaircraft guns, known as five-inch 38s. This weapon fired a shell that was furnished with a proximity fuse. This secret weapon, which took a heavy toll on attacking enemy planes, first came into use in very late 1942, during the Solomons campaign, and later became standard equipment on larger U.S. warships. The projectile exploded as it passed within approximately fifty feet (my observation) from the magnetic field of the target. It detonated into deadly steel fragments and a black cloud.

October 24, 1944, was certainly a most exciting day. U.S. Navy carrier planes intercepted the enemy air attack aggressively. We saw a dozen enemy planes either splashed or downed on shore. Off our starboard side, by the hatch of the wheelhouse, I saw a twin-engine Japanese bomber speeding directly toward us at an altitude of about sixty feet. All hell broke loose as

the wheelhouse that some sixty Japanese planes were headed to our area—the first important enemy air response to America's return. We were clearly in what could be called a hostile environment. The first order of the day was to make smoke in an effort to hide the ships from the approaching raiders. We watched as navy antiaircraft guns went after a single-engine Japanese

GI's watch as antiaircraft bursts follow a Japanese plane.

our gunners started firing. I remember wondering if we were about to end our work in San Pedro Bay. The plane just missed us, passing overhead with a deafening roar. I moved over to the port side but missed the bombing of what I figured was a seagoing tug. The plane then plunged into an LCI (landing craft, infantry), starting a large fire. I thought at the time that it was an in-tentional act. A few minutes earlier a Japanese plane had dived at a Liberty ship, just missing it. But the first planned suicide mission supposedly took place the next day.

The 49th's water echelon beached on schedule, at midday on the 24th, making the group, with its 7th, 8th, and 9th Fighter Squadrons, the first AAF air combat unit to move back into the

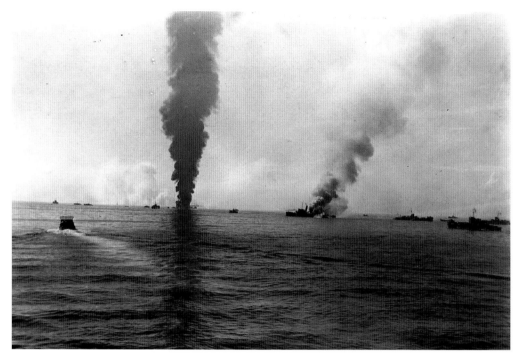

U.S. vessels burn in San Pedro Bay, off Leyte. Our gunners stand by. A twin-engine Japanese bomber had slammed into a landing craft just moments before.

Philippines. Our planes were to fly out of Tacloban airfield, a municipal airfield before the war that the Japanese had taken over as a secondary field. The main strip was more than a mile in length, while the east-west segment was much shorter and had been used by the enemy only for emergencies. We had plans to improve it considerably. Tacloban lay on the Cataisan Peninsula, a finger of land jutting into San Pedro Bay—just a short distance from many Japanese airstrips. For living space we were assigned to an area off Highway 1 in the Marasbora region, a bog that had been somewhat cleared. Night fell before we could set up tents or any shelter at all. I crawled under a truck in a hopeless attempt to escape the droves of mosquitoes, the likes of which I had never seen before or after. During the night, word spread like wildfire: "The Jap fleet is out there!"

The next day's legendary Battle for Leyte Gulf should take nothing away from the fierce time that the army's air

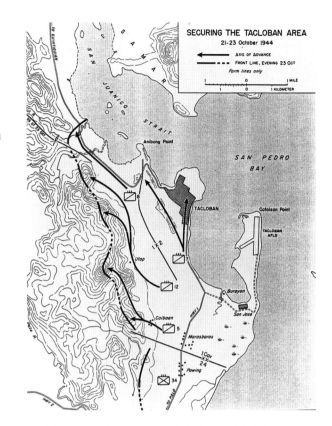

Tacloban, Leyte (Department of the Army, Chief of Military History).

and ground forces had in securing the island—or from the critical role of the air patch at Tacloban during the naval engagement. As the Japanese played havoc with our small carriers and escorts, navy fighters and bombers landed or crash-landed by the dozens on Tacloban's incomplete strip. Their carriers were either under Japanese guns or already sunk. The AAF's 305th Airdrome Squadron, with an assist from some of the 49th ground crews, rearmed and refueled some of the navy planes, which returned to harass the enemy's warships off the Island of Samar.

On the 26th, when the U.S. Navy started to withdraw its surviving planes from the area, I was ordered to the 7th FS as its communications officer. During the next several days we had one notable red alert that lasted for more than eighteen hours. In another twenty-four-hour period there were more than thirty strikes at and around our area. Shortly after midday on October 27, some three dozen P-38s buzzed the area, and then each landed on the still-unfinished airstrip. The flight was composed of the 7th and 9th Squadrons, with elements of the 8th arriving at Tacloban three days later. The Lightnings had flown up from Moratai. Our

7th Fighter Squadron suffered its first Philippine fatality on October 30. As a former FCS officer, I was especially regretful of the circumstances: Lieutenant Bob Searight, on early morning patrol, made an approach to land during a red alert and was shot down by friendly fire in his P-38. The Lightning went down into San Pedro Bay. About a week later a small navy landing craft returned his body to us.

During late October and into December, the enemy would attack in small numbers of three to five attackers. Many P-38s were either destroyed or seriously damaged on the strip. The Japanese flyers suffered their share of losses from antiaircraft fire as well as P-38 intercepts. But there was neither time nor facilities at Tacloban for any important repairs or maintenance in those hectic days. Damaged planes were literally shoved aside, some into the bay. As the struggle for air supremacy over Leyte continued, U.S. replacement aircraft were flown up from New Guinea. The Japanese, in turn, flew in new planes from Formosa. Establishing other bases—the U.S. planned a second operational strip at Dulag, about fourteen miles south of us—involved constant struggle against heavy rains, which left the roads impassable and halted construction. It was so muddy in our area that we moved the 49th camp about a half mile north. There the ground was a foot or two higher and gave us slightly better drainage.

Any veteran will testify that the devil (or God) is in the details. The first AAF single-engine American planes to arrive at Tacloban, a pair of unfamiliar P-47 Thunderbolts, suddenly appeared in early November, making what turned out to be an ill-advised, low-level, high-speed approach from north to south. As

A P-38 shoved aside at Tacloban strip.

Maj. Gerald R. (Jerry) Johnson's fifteen-plane scoreboard. The photo is admittedly flawed —some water spots on the negative marked the print, but more importantly there are blurs. I wanted to get the ace's scoreboard from an unusual angle, so I climbed up on the wing as an armorer worked on Johnson's weapons. At the instant the shutter clicked, antiaircraft guns cut loose at a Japanese plane. I shook, and the armorer jumped in a blur. In another "heroic moment" of mine, also involving Johnson, I climbed into a foxhole during the early days at Leyte and, to my surprise, found myself sharing it with a big snake, which I dispatched with two rounds from my 45. Before the echo of my second shot faded away, Johnson rushed out of his tent, clad in pajamas but with his 45 in hand, ready to take on the infiltrators.

The P-61 Black Widow at Tacloban, November 1944. The P-61 was the only aircraft the U.S. designed and built in WWII as a night fighter. It entered the SWPA in early 1944, mainly to replace the Douglas P-70 Havoc, which was an A-20 modified for night duty. Twin-engine Japanese nighttime raiders were easy prey for the P-61, but at Leyte many Japanese raids were composed of speedy and highly maneuverable single-engine fighter-bombers. On December 4, 1944, the 421st's P-61s were pulled off of night intercept duty and moved out. F-6F Hellcats of the 541st Marine Air Squadron replaced them. These radar-equipped planes proved effective against the Japanese night raiders. It was a black eye for the P-61 in the Philippines.

An Air Capital Transport Command Douglas c-54 Sky Master became the first big plane to land at the newly finished Tacloban strip, arriving the first week of November. It brought in some priority supplies and took out some wounded. We hoped that the shiny new c-54 would somehow escape enemy notice. The steel landing planks, known throughout World War II as Marston Mat (for the town in North Carolina near which it was first tested, in November 1941), proved essential in gaining air superiority in the late stages of the Pacific war. We even planked the short strip for use in the dispersal of planes.

they roared by, antiaircraft guns around the strip cut loose, and the Thunderbolts banked over the bay. One of them, hit, quickly rose, and I watched the pilot take to his parachute, which opened about two seconds before he hit the water. The crew of an LCM soon picked him up. The second P-47 headed over the bay toward Samar Island, followed by a series of five-inch 38s that formed black blasts to the rear of the plane. The P-47 trailed smoke, as the pilot, with good cause, pushed his throttle to war emergency power. When things settled down and we declared a cease-fire, he finally landed his plane safely. I chatted with both of the pilots. One was low on gas and could never have made it back to his base at Morotai. The other, who had headed for Samar, was literally shaking. Nearly sixty years later I can remember his exact words: "I was O.K. until those black cumulus clouds started following my plane!"

One late morning in mid-November we watched the aircraft belonging to

We found only one enemy plane at Tacloban, a Zero, and souvenir hunters made a shambles of it. Near the wreck, crewmen of the 8th FS ready P-38s for the next mission.

Major Richard Bong take off from north to south. With official credit for thirty-eight enemy planes shot down, Bong at the time led all pilots in the theater in air victories. We thought of him as an ace among aces. His plane became airborne but then quickly started to smoke, and in seconds it had plunged into the bay. We all thought we had seen the end of this American hero. Later that day, however, we found out that another pilot had borrowed Bong's plane for a mission. That was bad enough.

As time went on, the Japanese did most of their attacking during the early morning and late afternoon. Their planes did not come in large formations. Sometimes, instead of conventional raids at and around our strip, they would crash into ships in San Pedro Bay, kamikaze style. One morning my section chief and I were in a Jeep heading for the airfield when we observed a pair of Japanese Nicks headed our way at about four hundred feet. We stopped and dove into a shell

hole. As the planes passed over us, they were quickly followed by a pair of exploding five-inch 38 shells at the same altitude. Though exposed to the resulting friendly shrapnel shower, we ended up unhurt and thankful to be so.

In November I managed to take my

camera and visit some of the local landmarks in Tacloban, the provincial capital and Leyte's largest city. It had suffered very little damage and had been quickly liberated by the American forces. During the first days of the conflict the town's Roman Catholic church—mostly unscathed—served as a temporary shelter for the wounded. I also visited the Governor's Mansion, probably the most impressive dwelling on Leyte, nearly a mile from town. The Filipinos had spread palm leaves over

the roof, trying to camouflage it against Japanese aerial observation.

By December, the air power at Tacloban had grown impressively. Besides Hellcat night fighters equipped with radar, the base supported marine Corsairs, AAF Lightnings, and some Thunderbolts. There were also various navy and army bombers staging for raids against the enemy.

On December 12, 1944, General MacArthur paid Tacloban strip a visit to present Major Bong the Congressional Medal of Honor. We pulled three Lightnings over to the southwest dispersal area of the airfield for the ceremony. Around 10 A.M. Jim Gorse, 7th Squadron adjutant, rustled up a dozen officers for our section of the guard of honor. The 8th and 9th Squadrons furnished their own set of officers, all of us wearing our best khakis with a

A rather rare shot of a Lockheed P-V2 Harpoon. The navy used this twin-engine patrol plane for sea patrol and antisubmarine duties.

matching overseas cap and a shoulder holster with a 45 automatic. We all climbed aboard a weapons carrier (a midsized truck), quickly drove to the strip, and got into ranks for the presentation there. Soon the general's driver pulled up, and MacArthur got out of his Jeep. He wore his standard natty trench coat and visor cap. Bong, to our front, saluted smartly. From my position, I could hear none of the words that passed between the two men, but a dozen or so photographers made a record of the short event. MacArthur returned to his Jeep and left the scene.

Loading bombs onto an F-4U Corsair from MAG-12 (Marine Air Group 12). The unit busied itself attacking the many Japanese convoys reinforcing the Ormoc area of western Leyte.

I had to have my picture taken at Tacloban, and what better spot than beside this B-24, *Lady from Leyte*, staging through the strip.

We all took the cue and went on our way back to the duties at hand. Before being ordered back to the States for war bond sales and public relations work, Major Bong added two more kills to his record.

We had received no advanced notice of the award ceremony because Japanese air raids kept us on edge and security uppermost in mind. Six days earlier, the Japanese had pulled off an unusual attack. At dusk the enemy dropped more than two hundred airborne troops in the area south of Tacloban, where the United States recently had discontinued weather-hampered work on Burauen airfield. Tacloban strip remained a prime target. That same evening, as darkness fell, a Japanese plane got into the landing pattern at Tacloban and started its approach. Multiple 50-caliber antiaircraft guns fired and summarily shot it down. It crashed on the beach at the south end of the strip, killing some twenty-five demolitionists.

Around December 18, at midday, we had an unusual air show. A flight of four factory-fresh Japanese fighters (I figured that they were Georges) buzzed —flew fast and low over—the strip at about one hundred feet altitude, heading south to north, right over the landing mat. They were in loose formation, painted dark green with brilliant red national markings. They flew the length of the strip, headed out over the bay to Samar, and disappeared. I was right on the edge of the matting and at first thought it was a flight of p-47s coming in. What a surprise. Paradoxically, it was a beautiful scene—not a shot was fired by anyone.

The 49th Fighter Group received a Presidential Unit Citation for its work during the Leyte campaign.

LINGAYEN GULF

Christmas 1944 will remain fixed in my memory because on (or about) that day two of the 7th's sergeants and I boarded an unarmed and war-weary B-25 at Tacloban strip for the long journey—requiring a good number of refueling stops along the way—to Townsville, in northeast Australia. Orders for this TD (temporary duty) had the sound of serious business, and I still have them: "December 21, 1944. The fol named O and EM are placed on TD at (Station secret), will proceed thereto by mil acft o/a 25 December 1944 to carry out the instructions of the CO. Upon completion of TD will return to proper STA."

But the mission was basically R&R —a few days of change of scenery for us plus the assignment of picking up and returning with a few luxuries for the 7th, along the lines of food and drink. Bill Carlton and Sam Chiodo accompanied me; Walter Huckabee and his copilot, Jim McCrary, flew the 25. We reached our secret station in about three days, and from Townsville a short train ride took us to a little town called Ingham, where we stayed at the modest, but for us commodious, East Ingham Hotel. After a couple of days, the pilots left. We were to be picked up for the return to base later on, retracing our flight in a new C-47. This hop turned out to be longer in coming about than we had anticipated, and despite the comforts of Ingham, we soon got bored and antsy to leave. At last, after two or three weeks, our 47 appeared at Townsville, where it picked us up for our return to the front.

With our canned goodies and at least a short-term supply of scotch and gin, we finally reached the 49th FG's new base at Hill Field, Mindoro Island,

Campsite at Lingayen, with the gulf in the background.

about three hundred miles northwest of Leyte. We were actually glad to be in a forward area again. Unlike Leyte, this place was dusty and the land flat in the area where we camped. We knew our stay at Mindoro would be a short one. With no places of interest to visit, we spent our time either at the campsite or at the strip.

During the last week of February 1945, the 49th FG received orders to move again, this time another several hundred miles north, to Lingayen, on the west coast of the largest Philippine island, Luzon. Early on January 9, 1945, at Lingayen Gulf and along the shores of the South China Sea, U.S. forces had made their initial assault. We 49ers had arrived at the Lingayen airstrip totally by air, using either C-47s or C-46 Curtiss Commandos (I recall heavy preference for assignment to the highly trusted 47s). We left all vehicles and equipment at Mindoro, obtaining replacements at our new base. We also received a special bonus—a fine campsite that Filipino contractors had built and that another group had left behind. Between late February and early August 1945, the 49th never had it so good in terms of living conditions. As the war in Europe wound down, food and supplies continued to improve.

There were no daylight air attacks on our area, but sometimes at night one or two twin-engine intruders would come down from Formosa. Even if they caused little or no damage, the red alerts woke up a lot of airmen. As a general alarm, upon receiving orders from the control center, a designated

At Lingayen, the 7th Squadron's communication shack, along with the generator shelter, stood in the center of the 7th's dispersal area.

Typical quarters for the officers of the 49th FG. My tentmates at this juncture were pilots Dick Ganchan and Ray Kopecky, along with John Heartz, squadron intelligence officer. We had steps and even drop bamboo curtains, and we were a stone's throw from the waters of the Lingayen Gulf.

Bofors 40-millimeter antiaircraft gun would fire three rounds, which exploded high in the air. The warning shots could be heard for miles. One round signaled the all clear. During a red alert, no cigarettes could be smoked out in the open, and no lights of any kind could be used.

U.S. aviation engineers developed our strip at Lingayen, once a secondary

On the first two nights of the early January invasion at Lingayen, some seventy Japanese suicide boats from a surface raiding regiment attacked our ships off the beachhead. Heavily laden with explosives, the boats did their share of damage. We heard reports of two sunken U.S. ships. We also heard that the ships' defenses had been hampered by the simple fact that many guns did not depress below the horizontal — they could not fire directly at small boats at close range. For a period of time the 7th had two of these enemy craft. This one, captured by some 7th FS pilots, was the property of Bob Klemmedson, wearing a cap as the boat is being made ready for a runabout. These boats had been based at an inlet called Port Saul, and most of them met their end during this operation.

Japanese airstrip, into a first-rate field for more than a hundred and fifty fighters and some medium bomber outfits. Japanese aircraft had been eliminated or withdrawn from their Philippine bases entirely. Yet a few more aerial victories were added to the 49th's score. These came from fighter sweeps or bomber escorts to Hinan Island, Hong Kong, and Formosa.

American airmen in the Pacific theater followed a tradition honored by fighter pilots of every country's service —painting symbols of their kills on the fuselage of their planes. Of all the victory markings I saw, the trophies of Captain Louis E. Curdes stand out. A native of Fort Wayne, Indiana, Curdes during 1943 made his presence felt as a P-38 pilot in the Mediterranean theater.

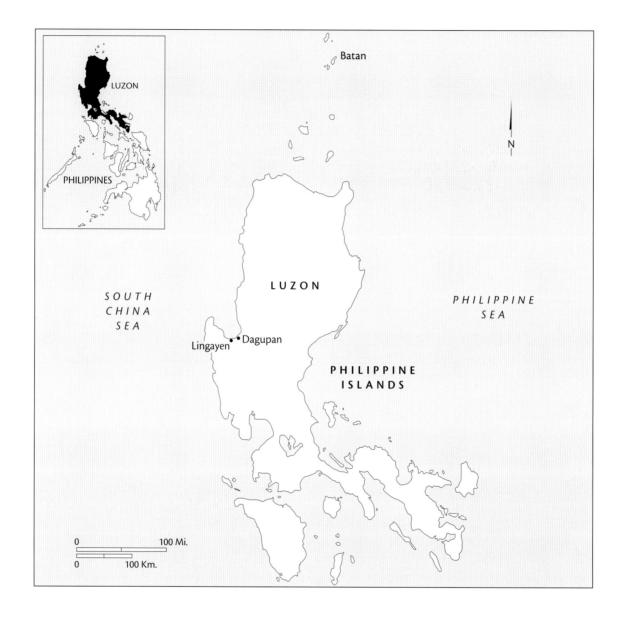

The 7th FS Communications Section. Left to right, front row: author (then communications officer), Klopinski, Pettyjohn, Scheckel, Kruger, Buria, Eggan, Nance, Groom. Second row: (bending over) Brokaw, Torrine, Humphreys, Belovouss, Dement. Standing: Chiodo, Clayton (Section Chief), Churilla, Schetel, Grobstein, Van Der Wurff, Redinger, Kamphendal, Mullen, Ball. Besides the diesel generator that supplied the camp with electricity, we were responsible for telephones and telephone lines and the P-38s' radios (Signal Corps Radio 522) and IFF (Identification Friend or Foe) equipment. When the squadron was at strength or full complement, we serviced as many as thirty-five aircraft, but the number typically was lower. The communications officer was appointed to be the IFF Officer and also the squadron's Cryptographic Security Officer.

Holding the line. Left to right are pilots Bill Bauer and Bill Franco Fernandez with Jim Gorse, 7th FS adjutant, about to be creamed. Jim said he could get through the two blockers, but a scouting report declared no way! The scrimmage may have followed what we called combat rations. After a mission debriefing, usually under supervision of the squadron's doctor, each pilot was issued two ounces of bourbon, often mixed with synthetic lemon juice. Some men put this allowance aside for a later occasion — to celebrate, if nothing else, life itself. The three squadrons of the 49th pooled resources and founded an "O," or Officer's Club.

A B-17 air-sea rescue plane code named *Jukebox* landed at Lingayen in March 1945. Besides being heavily armed, it carried a motorboat that was fully provisioned. The boat could be dropped by parachute to downed airmen. The USAAF did care about its men.

This North American P-51 Mustang belonged to the 110th Tactical Reconnaissance Squadron, which in the spring of 1945 replaced its P-40s with the 51s.

With its starboard engine out and prop feathered, this P-38 of the 8th Squadron nonetheless flew back to Lingayen and landed safely — a living example of why Pacific fighter pilots loved flying the P-38.

Damaged tail area of a B-25, late April 1945. This B-25's crewmen still have on their Mae Wests (life jackets). They had been on a skip-bombing training flight, the target a derelict Japanese ship. A practice missile hit the ship's deck and bounced up, striking the plane's rear. There was no tail gunner aboard and thus no casualties.

A Bunyap (the death head of Australian Aborigines) on the tail of a P-38. A few of the 7th FS P-38s had their tails adorned with Bunyaps. The 7th was known as the Screamin' Demons, the 8th as the Blacksheep, and the 9th as the Flying Knights.

A pair of Grumman Avengers paid a short visit to our field in April 1945. U.S. Navy lieutenant George H. W. Bush flew an Avenger until he was shot down at sea and rescued by a lifeguard submarine.

A P-38 in dispersal at Lingayen strip. Through the spring of 1945, our P-38s had a white band around the prop's hub and a white-tipped nose. The principal color for the 7th was a bright blue.

Nine men of the 7th FS on a Jeep at the beach at Lingayen Gulf. Left to right, front: George Spruell Jr. (one victory), Fernley Damstrom (eight victories), and Dick Ganchan. Behind them are Jim Keck (one victory) and Dwight Henderson (one victory). Back row: myself, Louis Denkovic, Charles Garrett, and Jim Jarrell (four victories). Several members of this group soon lost their lives, though not to

enemy action. About two weeks later Damstrom died in an operational accident. He and wingman Sylvan Sisson had flown to north Luzon to a re-captured secondary airstrip at Laoag. The purpose of the mission was to intercept a Japanese two-engine intruder that came down from Formosa to harass our area on many nights. The idea had been to knock it out on its return flight, at first light, but the unit called off the mission after several days' work without luck. Starting home, Damstrom lost an engine on takeoff. His P-38 ran out of strip, pitched over, and killed the ace.

Far worse to tell, in early May, after a short sup-port mission, the eight-plane squadron com-menced a "rat race"—a game of follow the leader through steep climbs and dives, tight turns, and so on—about a half mile offshore from our camp. As I watched from my tent, I saw the game break down, with the P-38s milling around randomly. I called to tentmate John Heartz to "come here and see this mess!" Just as Heartz got by my side, two Lightnings hit head-on at high speed, ending the lives of George Rogers and Lou Denkovic. We considered it an awful accident rather than a breach of discipline, because fighter pilots had to keep a sharp edge and, in any case, had to be willing to take chances, even in intramural dog-fights. They were "like that"—making the loss, by classical definition, tragic.

When one looks at photographs taken during the war on Luzon, most depict nothing but the violence, suffering, and damage in Manila. With a little time to spare, I took a few shots around Lingayen, one of them of the first helicopter I had ever seen, a Sikorsky R-4. It had landed at an open field near a school, and I never quite got a clear view, because every time I did attempt a shot, a crowd of kids moved in front of the camera. They in fact make the scene far more interesting.

Other scenes from the locale demonstrate the simplicity of life there, even in 1945. Small boats, horses, and oxen played important parts in transportation and the local economy. Remnants of Spanish rule could dominate a crossroads setting. It was a peculiar world, and sometimes I wonder what has happened to these people and their ways since then.

His varied career included going down at sea in his 38. In January 1945 Curdes, then a lieutenant and a P-51 pilot, entered the Pacific war and was based at Mangaldan field, just east of Lingayen. On May 24 he was assigned to the 49th FG and three days later was on the roster of the 8th FS.

Curdes's aircraft carried symbols of victories over German, Italian, and Japanese pilots, making his plane a subject of much admiration. But the question so often arose, "What the heck is the story on that American marking?" The story traces to the middle of February 1945, when Curdes flew over Formosa as a member of a four-plane sweep (downing one Japanese plane). On the way home, the flight decided to do a little work on the small island of Batan. This enemy-held island (not to be confused with Bataan, the site of a death march the victorious Japanese forced the defenders of Corrigidor to make in early 1942) was located about 150 miles north of Luzon. Curdes and the others hit an airfield

114

Close side view of scoreboard of Curdes's P-51, *Bad Angel*, taken while Curdes was on a 49th FG visit at Lingayen in April 1945.

known as Basco strip. During the attack ground fire hit one of the Mustangs, and a few minutes later an American pilot was floating around in a rubber dinghy. One of the 51s headed high to send out an SOS and a fix, while the other two headed home for help.

Circling low in a protective pattern, Curdes spotted a C-47 heading to Batan, apparently believing the airstrip

In late May 1945, over a three-day stay, the comic film star Joe E. Brown (best known for his strutting Elmer the Great routine) entertained 49ers at Lingayen and later posed next to a P-38 flown by Gerald R. "Jerry" Johnson (then CO of the 49th FG). Evenually credited with twenty-two kills, Jerry Johnson also had several probables. The Aussie emblem in the center of his score did not reappear on his later P-38s. Back in the New Guinea days, he had downed an Aussie Boomerang, thinking it was an enemy plane (the pilot survived without serious injury). Brown autographed the 7th Squadron's Pilots' Status Board under the supervision of Oliver "Atch" Atchison, who won two confirmed victories and two probables during the Leyte show.

Left to right, ace Fred Dick with Jim Keck and Capt. Richard "Dick" Ganchan. (ABOVE, RIGHT) Jim Costley poses by his P-38, *Winnie*.

Dick Ganchan (in coveralls) with his crew chief. The painting (of Ganchan's wife) was done by Bob Klemmedson with oil paints. Bob Helfrecht, on a mission in late June, was lost without a trace off Luzon flying this P-38, *Southern Miss*.

The 7th's leading ace, Bob DeHaven, flew this custom-decorated P-38. DeHaven won ten victories around New Guinea in P-40s and, in a P-38, four more around Leyte.

Almost 'a' Draggin'. Major Isaacson, having finished a European tour of duty, came to the Pacific and, for a short time in mid-1945, served as CO of the 7th. In July, Ray Kopecky, a tentmate, became CO for a few weeks, relieving Isaacson.

With the shell-torn provincial capitol in the background, a four-engine, heavily armed navy PB4Y2 Privateer taxis and then prepares to lift off after a stopover at Lingayen strip. In our theater a Privateer was a rare bird.

A dozen P-38s of the 8th FS neatly parading on Lingayen's taxiway. The 38s were using napalm canisters, and the target was a Japanese stronghold on northern Luzon.

In June 1945, I displayed my "short snorter" string of money. As I recall, a short snorter was someone who had flown over a foreign country, was more or less a good guy, and had enough money to buy a fellow a drink. My string of bills included signatures of friends and associates, as well as the signatures of ten aces and a few other luminaries.

to be under U.S. control. Curdes felt he had to intervene, lest the transport and all aboard fall into enemy hands. Unable to make radio contact with the C-47 or any American base nearby, he shot out one, then two, of the plane's engines, sending the C-47 into a water landing. He flew over the scene long enough to notice a dozen Americans, including nurses, in the rubber raft.

Reynaldo Perez Gallardo, a pilot from the Mexican squadron.

A Douglas A-20G Strafer stops over at Lingayen strip, July 1945.

He headed home, having done all he could, good or bad. The story ends well. The next morning he and a wingman flew out at daybreak to cover the rescue of the Americans. As the 51s circled protectively over the downed people, a PBY Catalina picked them all up, including the downed Mustang pilot. The pilot of the C-47 had indeed expected to land on Basco strip. Curdes actually won the Distinguished Flying Cross for shooting down one of our own C-47s.

GIs affectionately called the P-47 the Jug, and those of the 201st Mexican Fighter Squadron of the Mexican Ex-peditionary Air Force (MEAF) naturally were called El Jarro Mexicano. Many in the United States never knew that there was such a thing as the MEAF in the war against Japan. The 201st reached Clark Field in April and worked with the American 58th FG, lending support to American ground troops on Luzon. It obtained its P-47s from some American squadrons that were converting to the P-51. In early July, one plane from the Mexican squadron with fuel problems paid our strip a visit after a fighter sweep over Formosa. While the Mexican insignia was used on some of the P-47s, this

In July, mainly to ward off boredom, a group of us ventured into Manila, visiting the house once occupied by the secretary to the country's vice president — a lovely place with a miniature pagoda in the garden and, we thought, an exotic interior courtyard — and paying a call at nearby Nichols Field, where we found remnants of a Nakajima-made Helen, a Japanese medium bomber, among other debris.

one retained U.S. markings. Its rudder, however, sported the red, white, and green of the Mexican flag. I spent an hour or so chatting (in simple English) with the pilot, Reynaldo Perez Gallardo. When he taxied away for takeoff, heading on to Clark Field, I threw him a salute—and he tossed me a thumbs-up.

The practice of personalizing aircraft according to the whims of crewmen developed into an art form by the end of the war. I found the paintings rich subjects for my camera. Collected together (and not necessarily from planes based at Lingayen alone), the images say something of the bravado, the humor, and, of course, the loneliness of the airmen in the Pacific war.

MOTOBU, OKINAWA

In August 1945, the 49th Fighter Group again divided into two parts, water and air echelons, for the move from Lingayen to Okinawa, a distance of about eight hundred miles. The water echelon left during the first week of the month, while the air echelon waited at Lingayen for the completion of Motobu strip, our next 49er base. We wanted for nothing in the new campaign. Since the surrender of Germany in May, supplies had truly been pouring into the Pacific. The 7th FS received many new P-38s, reaching our Table of Equipment level of thirty-five, along with some extra pilots.

We of the 7th and some 49th head-quarters people sailed aboard LST 530, one of about eight vessels in our group. We knew that the 49th was being groomed for the assault against Japan and was reportedly scheduled to be the first AAF group to be based in the Home Islands. We viewed the assignment as potentially hazardous, to say the least. The flotilla was well under-

LST 452, seen through a porthole.

While waiting for what we hoped would be the official announcement of a cease-fire, our naval contingent combated boredom by offering short local cruises, shipping passengers on an LCVP (landing craft, vehicle / personnel) from our flotilla. On one of the trips, beer aboard, suntans in evidence, Jim Benson (USNR), with his back to the camera, tries fishing — and caught a few. Bill Lilly (USNR), far left, in white shirt, put on a nonissue painter's cap, and, to the right, Jim Gorse, 7th FS adjutant, wears a smile as if the war was over. "Doc" Canter, D.D.S., and Jake Shelman of Squadron Headquarters stand in front of them. I'm sitting on the left, having finished my beer. Lieutenant (jg) Seiders (USNR) has the helm. With him, far right, is George "Doc" Webster, the 7th Squadron's surgeon.

way when we got radio reports of two great bombs dropped on Japan. Rumors of peace followed.

When we arrived at Okinawa, we anchored off the Motobu Peninsula near the small island of Sesoke-Shima and remained resting at anchor in the harbor. With no formal announcement of a cease-fire, we continued to darken the ships at night and more or less kept ourselves combat ready.

On Wednesday, August 15, 1945, at 0800 Tokyo time, the United States and Japan agreed to a cease-fire. The big

Lieutenant Duke's smile expresses the relief all of us felt on hearing news of the cease-fire.

Okinawa — Heart of the Nansei Shoto (Intelligence Summary No. 265, Headquarters, Allied Air Forces, S.W.P.A, ca. August 1945). Just 9 by 13 inches in size, this map may be one of the most detailed depictions of Okinawa and its environs made up to that time. Pen-and-ink additions of the Ruby Tower and Plum Tower (on Ie Shima) aided navigation. Following the 314 line (upper left, pointing south-eastward) from Plum leads to Tekugi (we called it Toguchi), where we set up. We were to establish the new Motobu airstrip nearby.

128

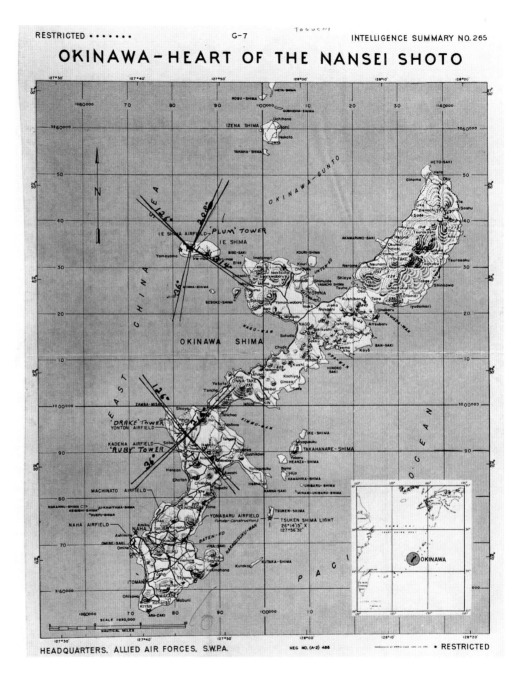

A 7th FS P-38 landing at Motobu. This end of the strip began abruptly — at the edge of a sheer cliff some 125 feet in height, so for most pilots landing at Motobu was a new experience. They approached the strip as if attempting a carrier landing; all we lacked was an LSO (landing signal officer) to guide them in.

war's shooting had ended. Five minutes after the welcome word reached us, the skipper of LST 530, Lieutenant A. D. Duke, invited me to join him at the highest place on his ship for a quiet celebration. We had only that moment to savor the long-awaited arrival of peace, however, for later that day the 49th water echelon beached and proceeded to set up temporary camp. A day or two after we came ashore, eighty-five P-38s of the 49th landed safely on the brand-new airstrip. Along with the offshore strip on Ie Shima,

A sunken Japanese submarine tender of about ten thousand tons, a victim of U.S. Navy planes, protrudes from the water off the Motobu Peninsula.

The sizable town of Nago lay only a few miles from Motobu, and eventually a few of us — myself along with section chief Wayne Dement, Bethel Nance, and Andy Kruger — took the communications Jeep over for a quick look. We went as we were, and one can observe that in the Fifth AAF there was no dress code in forward areas. "Get the job done right" was the order of the day. The sign posted as traffic entered Nago speaks for itself — in more than one language.

(BELOW) Motobu was a busy airstrip for a time, serving planes of the army, navy, and marines. Here, in late August 1945, C-46s line up on the taxiway while B-24s stand in dispersal. Unlike most other airfields on Okinawa, aviation engineers had literally "scratched it out" of the rugged terrain.

Enterprising laundry ladies set up a service and helped keep us neat and tidy.

Motobu supplied the closest airfields to Japan's Home Islands. At this point, the 49ers had orders to make armed surveillance flights over Japan's southern islands.

Soon I ventured out with my camera to see the place so many Americans had died to capture for us. Destruction was everywhere. Among the Okinawan people (linguistically Japanese but independent of Japan until the 1870s—and proud of their provincial culture), the youngsters, especially the boys,

Jake Shelman with eleven Sesoke-Shima boys, who relished lining up for a photo. (ABOVE) Bashful Okinawan girls, with various expressions.

Designed to replace the Douglas A-20, this twin-engine Douglas attack plane, the A-26, saw

132 service late in the war. Shortly afterward the *A* was dropped, and its designation became the B-26 Invader — as if the Martin A-26 Marauder had never existed.

Here a three-blade propeller F-4U Corsair sits in dispersal, with Motobu's rugged terrain in the background.

Parking space at times could be scarce, but the pilot of this four-bladed prop Corsair knew how to handle the problem. This version was equipped with a very high horsepower engine and was considered by some observers to be the best fighter plane any nation employed in World War II. I had seen it in mock dogfights with other American fighters, and the four-bladed Corsair ruled.

Besides the famous P-38, one other twin-engine, single-seat U.S. fighter served in the Pacific — the navy (or marine) Grumman F-7F2, known as the Tigercat and surely a rare bird. The marine pilot of this one, with whom I chatted briefly, informed me that there was also a two-seat version, the F-7F2N, primarily a night fighter. Coral dust fills the air as the Tigercat prepares to take to the runway.

seemed friendly enough. The post-invasion situation being grim, women gladly took wages as laundresses.

In addition to our fighters, Motobu strip provided a home to a group of B-24s, whose billboardlike sides invited especially ambitious nose art—the subject as usual being women from home in various states of undress. I took a few more pictures for posterity. There were some talented artists in the Pacific, but, if I were to judge, whoever created *Daisy Mae* took best of show.

On August 26 the front page of the Fifth AAF newsletter, the *Invader*, announced the landing, in Japan, of two

P-38s—the first U.S. aircraft to put down peaceably on Japanese soil since before Pearl Harbor. The article did not mention details, but the plane belonged to a 7th FS armed-surveillance mission of eight aircraft, led by the 49th commanding officer, Lieutenant Colonel Clay Tice, who in July had relieved Jerry Johnson for service in higher headquarters. Tice had two confirmed victories, one in the defense of Darwin, Australia, in a P-40, and another during the Battle of Bismarck Sea.

Colonel Tice's mission report to the 49th Fighter Group explained that the episode had followed after one plane in the patrol had encountered a fuel problem. There being no sign of enemy antiaircraft fire over the course of the flight, Tice had decided, rather than losing the aircraft and taking a chance on losing the pilot by ditching at sea, to land on the Japanese field at Nittagahara and call for assistance from a B-17 of the 6th Air Sea Rescue Squadron. A little after 1 P.M., about an hour after landing, some officers and men of the Japanese army appeared, Tice reported. Although conversation was difficult, the pilots were greeted in a friendly manner. The B-17 landed within minutes. With the help of a fuel

Just a day after Colonel Tice landed in Kyushu, men of the 7th work on *Elsie*, his noteworthy Lightning. The prop's hub displays a spiral pattern of orange and purple-blue. The P-38s that Tice flew all had the skull and war hatchet motif on the engine nacelles as well.

pump and hose that the Japanese furnished, the Americans reloaded the tanks of the nearly dry P-38 and took off, reaching home by about 4 P.M. The culprit turned out to a faulty cross valve in the plane, which had made it impossible to switch from empty to full tanks. "Instructions in all details of the fuel system and gas consumption characteristics of the P-38 will now be given and will be followed by actual demonstrations and written examinations by all pilots of this organization," Tice concluded. His landing may have been historic, but it also represented a screw-up. "All efforts will be made to prevent any possible reoccurrence of this situation either by pilot error or mechanical failure" (from the copy of report in my possession).

Many years later, at a unit reunion, I learned that Tice and his fellow Americans had noticed a couple of Tony fighters parked by the strip at Kyushu, and Tice had had his eye on one of these in case he needed to borrow a plane. Soon some Japanese army personnel came onto the scene, including an English-speaking junior officer. The young officer saluted the colonel, who, realizing the nature of the moment, returned the military courtesy. Before long the town's mayor showed up on a bicycle. He was dressed in a morning suit, with striped pants topped off by a black silk opera hat. The mayor offered to surrender his town to Tice, but the colonel told him he was not in the position to accept at the time. Getting safely home, with his American associates, was his highest priority.

After being stationed on Okinawa for about three weeks, the 49th Fighter Group again broke up into air and water echelons (although the occupation of the Home Islands had all the earmarks of a peaceful operation). A few days later we left Motobu (APO 337) behind.

TOUCHDOWN AT ATSUGI

The air echelon, led by Colonel Tice, included thirty-six p-38s and elements of all squadrons, the 7th, the 8th, and the 9th; it departed Motobu on September 8 and landed at Atsugi, just a short distance from Tokyo, where MacArthur had first set foot on Japanese soil. The planes flew armed but without ammunition, the war officially being over as of September 2. We filled the ammo trays with K rations and other supplies; each Lightning carried a sleeping cot. Orders were issued to stow away sidearms, so all pilots landed completely unarmed. On their first night at Atsugi, the pilots slept either in their planes or on their cots, under a wing. The next day these first arrivals received assignment to barracks a mile or two from the airfield. Atsugi Naval Air Station had been considered the most important airfield in the Tokyo

To my knowledge, the first stowaway aboard an LST during the Pacific war. Patrol Craft 466 approaches our LST's port side.

Crewmen on the bow of the USS *Pasadena* watch our small convoy of LSTs ease through Tokyo Bay, headed for Yoko-hama. A light cruiser of the *Cleveland* class, the heavily armed *Pasadena* carried two observation planes.

Light fog enhances this view of the handsome bat-tleship HMS *King George V,* flagship of the British Pacific Fleet.

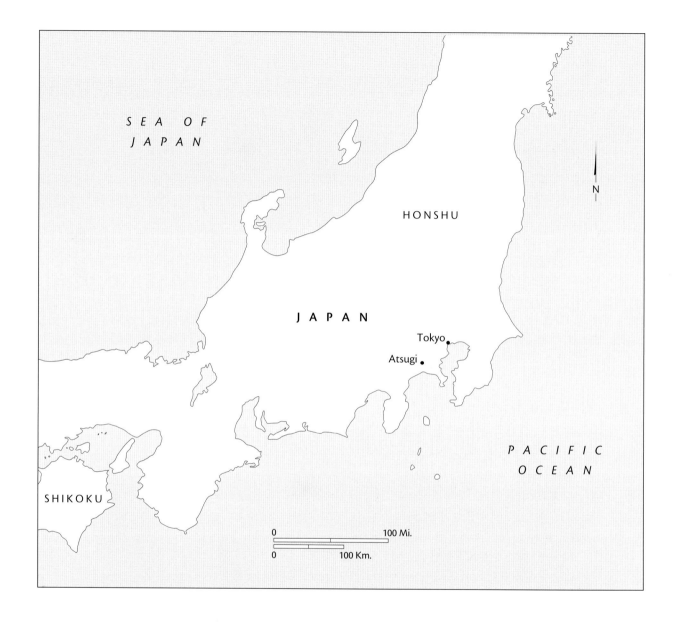

SEA OF JAPAN

HONSHU

JAPAN

Tokyo

Atsugi

SHIKOKU

PACIFIC OCEAN

N

0   100 Mi.

0   100 Km.

region. The base was stocked with more than three hundred Japanese navy airplanes of various types.

On September 9, "Atch" Atchison, as flight leader, with seven other P-38 pilots, was ordered to go to nearby Chofu, formerly a Japanese army fighter base and home to several dozen Tony and Frank fighters. Atchison's detachment arrived at Chofu that afternoon and found the place totally abandoned. In effect, Atch served as temporary base commander. Our eight fighter pilots took over some of the Japanese officer quarters, enjoying many fortunes-of-war luxuries. On the second day there, a low-flying B-29 dropped more supplies to sustain the airmen, who agreed that they never had it so good on overseas duty.

Assigned to the water echelon, I, along with the 7th Squadron and the headquarters people, left about September 8 and beached at Yokohama a few days later. The trip was easy; we had moved up to Japan in a small convoy made up of six LSTs accompanied

A well-armed, late-model Zero, shoved aside, with U.S. transports in the background.

by two sub chasers. We of the 7th Squadron and Group Headquarters traveled aboard LST 878. There was no zigzagging, so we moved along, wasting no time. There was also no nighttime blackout. With the war over, we could actually enjoy the cruise. When our small convoy moved off the shores of Japan, we were picked up by a patrol craft with a pilot aboard. The pilot led us from Sagami Bay into Tokyo Bay. The day was hazy, but we were still able to see many Allied warships at anchor.

By mid-September, our whole group had arrived at Atsugi, and the 49ers became the first Army Air Force combat unit based in Japan. Perhaps we had received some sort of honor; we were reputed to be MacArthur's favorite fighter group. In any case, we put up our weather-beaten sign in the group's living area, a former Japanese spot, along with a Fifth Air Force insignia. At least for a few days, all flight activity consisted of C-46 transports and our 49th FG P-38s. One of the C-46 Curtiss Commandos, I noted, had fulfilled its "Tokyo or Bust" pledge. The same plane had caught my eye several times earlier, as it went about its work in the Philippines. Only color film could have captured its superb artwork, but film of any kind was scarce, and I had to be satisfied with black and white. "Tokyo" appeared in a deep red,

while "or Bust" glowed in primary yellow. The flesh and makeup of the painted lady were admirably natural in appearance; her hair was jet black and her sparse garb a flaming red. Its pilot, Wayne K. Swarts, had grown up in Lansing, Michigan.

From our perspective, the occupation of Japan proceeded commendably. The Japanese military's cooperation exceeded expectations. At the Atsugi air base, hundreds of warplanes had been rendered inoperative, usually by removal of the propellers. The Japanese had handled everything of this kind before the American takeover, as part of the surrender terms. By the time we 49ers moved in there was no Japanese military presence; they had abandoned the area completely.

In ways large and small, we soon saw what the war had done to Japan. At what we called the boneyards, we bulldozed Japanese aircraft into heaps for destruction and to make room for Allied planes. These scenes of wrecked

A small Japanese suicide plane at Chofu. This little-known Japanese suicide plane — a Nakajima ĸ1-115 Tsurgi Sword — was built for a one-way combat sortie. The fuselage had a cavity for a large bomb. The undercarriage was jettisoned upon takeoff on a mission. We heard that the Japanese constructed only about one hundred of them; there were no reports of its combat use. Jim Costley and Bob Wecker look it over.

The infamous Baka (Fool) suicide flying bomb in a covered revetment at Atsugi. These guided-missile-like weapons, flown by a kamikaze pilot, were released from Betty bombers when the bomber crew made visual contact with American ships. Radar allowed U.S. Navy fighters to intercept the bombers early, and virtually all efforts by the enemy went for naught.

At Chofu, I caught a glimpse of a prototype of the Nakajima K1-87 high-altitude interceptor. A large and impressive-looking aircraft, it was akin to the highly regarded Frank fighter, one of the war's best combat craft. This plane was tagged and set aside for evaluation by the AAF.

Victory markings — each symbolizing a B-29—on the fuselage of a dead Tony at Chofu.

Our Jack in a covered revetment.

A small bulldozer moving Jack to a safer area.

Our Jack in a roofless hangar.

and captured aircraft clearly reflected the enormity of Japan's defeat.

For a short while I was part of the capturing detail for the 49th, making me part owner of a Mitsubishi Raiden (Thunderbolt) J-2M3, code-named Jack. Some pilots of the 49th, as well as ground crewmen, admired the design and the quality of this fighter. We decided that a Jack must be saved and restored to flight status. At one edge of Atsugi's base we found one, almost flight worthy, in a covered revetment. We "captured" this one and determined to save it from the scrap heap.

Less expansive views capture the meaning of the moment, sometimes even more dramatically than scrapped Zeros and tamed Tonys and the like. Near Chofu I happened to come across a little Japanese boy who, upset at something he saw, seemed to have reached understanding beyond his years — as indeed had many of us.

Seven of the 49th "early birds" pose for a picture before heading home. Left to right, rear: Charles Manion, author, and Don Spindler; front: Jim Flowers, Bob Wecker, Jim Costley, and Larry Sievers.

(LEFT) Junior officers' living quarters at Atsugi. Each unit had two sections sheltering two officers. (RIGHT) In the countryside near Atsugi air base, a former Japanese soldier does some bartering with Jim Costley and Larry Sievers, who plan to exchange a pack of Camels for something despite the language barrier. The woman looking on offers a priceless look of amusement. I can say that I never saw any display of hostility or arrogance toward the occupying forces.

Bob Klemmedson took this shot of me and some little friends who often visited me. All of us reflect the happiness we share at peace.

On the Road to Tokyo.

ROUTE
2S
TOKYO

YOU ARE NOW ENTERING
TOKYO
Courtesy
of
1st CAVALRY DIVISION
The First Team
FIRST IN MANILA   FIRST IN TOKYO

A volunteer bulldozer operator went to work. This early phase of Operation Save a Jack was a success. The plane stood safely in a roofless hangar. Next thing would be the total restoration of this plane. But then headquarters handed down an order forbidding unauthorized flights in any Japanese aircraft. The project never recovered.

It was my good fortune to be able to Jeep into Tokyo twice in that September shortly after war's end, traveling with Ray Kopecky, Atch Atchison, and Doc Webster. Both visits, needless to say, proved memorable. Many areas in and around Tokyo were completely in shambles—the devastation the work not so much of high explosives as the fire-bombing raids B-29s conducted late in the war. In some places the odor of death still permeated the air.

And yet a good portion of Tokyo came through the war unscathed. The business areas of the city were in remarkably good condition. It struck me that some of the buildings and streetscapes resembled those of Washington,

A Buddha statue sits amid the war's destruction in Tokyo—another witness to Japan's defeat.

D.C. The people themselves supplied rich subjects, especially in these circumstances. When we stopped the Jeep, the Japanese would quickly come to look us over in peaceful curiosity. Some shots just begged to be taken, like one of a darling little girl beside an already busy souvenir stand. We expected to see sailors on shore leave enjoying the sights in Tokyo and

The entrance to a park, probably a Shinto shrine, in

the suburbs of Tokyo.

Dolls everywhere! Samurai kitsch for occupying troops.

Downtown Tokyo scene about ten days after the surrender. U.S. military vehicles make up most of what little traffic there is.

Army trucks park along a tree-shaded, undamaged street.

Newspapers in Tokyo mostly unavailable, Tokyo residents
relied on public bulletin boards.

We lunched at the famous Imperial Palace Hotel,
which taught me that I preferred GI rations.

(ABOVE) Guards at the main entrance of the Emperor's Palace Grounds. At right, another view of the Emperor's palace.

Doc Webster views the Emperor's Palace moat. It was the fighter pilot's ambition before going home to shoot down a Jap plane. The ambition of the ground crewman, generally less known, was to piss in the Emperor's moat. I had this golden opportunity but must confess I abstained.

admiring the young women, but we did not expect to find such smiling resilience among the people. The most astonishing sight of all may have been a softball game in a Tokyo park, American sailors playing against former Japanese soldiers, surrounded by watchful fans, all of it taking place maybe two weeks after the formal surrender.

During the first weeks at Atsugi our pilots took their P-38s on some orientation flights, but by October the Lightnings mainly sat parked at the field

Boys near the base, one of them obviously a "character."

on standby. While most of our thoughts were about going home, living conditions for us were not at all bad. We were located well out in the country, near a few small settlements. Probably the only complaint heard—and the toughest thing for us to get used to—was the environment. I mean specifically the so-called country air. The farmlands were fertilized in the most primitive fashion. Our clothing had been totally tropical issue, and it was not until October 20 that we each received a set of woolens—one shirt and one pair of trousers. There were plenty of colds among those of us who had spent so much time in the tropics. By October the food was the best we had seen overseas. Besides, we were using a mess hall and not a tent. Movies—good ones such as *Going My Way, Shine on Harvest Moon,* and *Along Came Jones*—were shown on Tuesdays, Thursdays, and Saturdays.

EPILOGUE

In the second week of October, my friend Charles Manion replaced me as the 7th's communications officer, and on October 23 I followed my long-awaited orders and reported to the 11th Replacement Battalion at Itrumagawa. These units consisted of nothing more than clerks processing several thousands of the happiest men in the world—those who were going stateside. We soon headed to our port of embarkation, Yokohama, where we climbed aboard the USS *General George M. Randall* (AP 115), destined for Tacoma, Washington.

Not quite loaded to the gunwales (gunnels) as had been the *John Pope*

The Rotarians came out to greet us as we neared Tacoma. The flag beneath the banner was composed of colored lights for night operations.

when it took us overseas, the *Randall,* we learned, would take the Great Circle Route—the shortest, most direct way between two points on the world's spherical surface. We headed into the cold North Pacific for the nine- or ten-day journey, which proved uneventful. Except for cold air on the weather decks, living conditions during the crossing were rather pleasant—the food was plentiful and not at all bad. We were permitted to take aboard ship only what we could carry, and I had managed two full barrack bags. Such was my sense of relief or release, however—or simply weariness at having toted one's worldly goods around the Pacific for so many months—that I decided to shuck some of the weight. Lots of items went overboard, and my burden grew much lighter. When I disembarked at Tacoma, I had but one bag—and no plans to remain in the military.

Next, we troops from the East Coast climbed aboard railroad coaches, pulled by a steam locomotive, for the four-day ride across the country. Conditions were scarcely comfortable, but no one complained a word that I heard. For myself, after spending more than three years in uniform, two of them overseas, thoughts of surviving the war and going home were the balm of the trip.

After all these years, the uneventfulness of it all seems remarkable. We had participated in one of the great

A Burlington railroad coach bearing the effects of GI sarcasm. Lieutenant Robert Boniece, 49th FG, poses for one last shot.

struggles in history—and one of the most important, because it preserved, and set the world on a course for, democracy. Now we citizen-soldiers were demonstrating why, on one level, we had prevailed. We only wanted to get home.

I arrived at Fort Meade, Maryland, for mustering out on November 24, 1945, and met my family the next day, my journey finally over.

INDEX

Page numbers in **bold** refer to photographs.

A-20 (Douglas Strafer), 19, 92, **120**, 132

A-24 (Douglas Dauntless), 79

A-26, 132

A-35 (Vultree Vengeance), 61

Atchison, Oliver "Atch," **115**, 143, 153

B-17 (Flying Fortress), 31, 108

B-24 (Liberator): decoration of, 100, 135, **135**; deployment of, 31, **31**; at U.S. air bases, 19, 30, **74**, **75**, **130**

B-25 (Mitchell): decoration of, 27, 29; description of, 28; redeployment of, 31; at U.S. air bases, 19, 28, 69, **78**, 109

B-26 (Douglas Invader), **132**

B-26 (Martin Maurauder): description of, 19, 22; first combat missions of, 21; nicknames of, 21, 26; replacement of, 132; speed of, 26–28

B-29, 153

Baka (Fool) suicide flying bombs, 146

Bauer, Bill, 107

Beam, George, **52**

Benson, Jim, 127
Bong, Maj. Richard, 96, 98–100
Boniece, Lt. Robert, 165
Boomerang, 60, 61
Boyle, Bill, 40
Bristol Beaufighter, 76
Bristol Beaufort, 16, 55–56
Brown, Irby C., 12
Brown, Joe E., 115
Bush, Lt. George H. W., 110

C-46 (Curtiss Commando), 103, 130, 144, 144–45
C-47 (Douglas Dakota, Skytrain), 16, 19, 58, 103
C-54 (Douglas Sky Master), 94
Canter, "Doc," 127
Carlton, Bill, 102
Chicoski, Stanley, 49, 54
Chiodo, Sam, 102
Costley, Jim, 116, 146, 149, 150
Curdes, Capt. Louis E., 105, 114, 120–21, 114

Damstrom, Fernley, 111
DeHaven, Robert M. "Bob," 26, 117
Dement, Wayne, 130
Denkovic, Louis, 111
Dick, Fred, 116
Duke, Lt. A. D., 127, 129

8th Fighter Squadron (Blacksheep), 49th Fighter
    Group, 81, 90, 110, 119

F-4U (Corsair), 98, 99, 132, 133
F-6F Hellcat, 59, 60, 92, 98

F-7F2 (Grumman Tigercat), 134
Fernandez, Bill Franco, 107
58th Fighter Group, 121
541st Marine Air Squadron, 92
Flowers, Jim, 149
40th Division, U.S. Army, 58
49th Fighter Group, 26; deployment of, 83–89,
    102–3, 126–27, 129, 138, 143–44; reputation of,
    34, 73, 101
408th Bombardment Squadron, 22d Bomber
    Group, 19
475th Fighter Group, 31–34
432d Fighter Squadron, 475th Fighter Group, 32

Gallagher, Lt. James, 26, 54, 65–66, 73, 100, 119,
    127, 149, 150, 163–65
Gallardo, Reynaldo Perez, 120, 124
Ganchan, Capt. Richard "Dick," 104, 111, 116
Garrett, Charles, 111
General George Randall, USS, 163–64
General John Pope, USS, 5–7
George (Japanese fighter), 101
Glenn L. Martin (Martin Aircraft), 19, 22, 26
Gorse, Jim, 98, 107, 127
Grumman Avenger, 110

Haley, Sgt. Jim, 65
Harlan, Joe, 20
Heartz, John, 104, 111
Helen (Japanese bomber), 123
Helfrecht, Bob, 116
Henderson, Dwight, 111
Hornbaker, Fletcher, 73

Huckabee, Walter, 102
Huey, Wing, **49**

Isaacson, Major, 117

Japanese landing barges, **17**
Jarrell, Jim, **111**
Johnson, Maj. Gerald R. (Jerry), 90, **115**
Johnson, Lt. Stu, 66
Jones, Cyril, **15**

Keck, Jim, **111**, 116
King George V, HMS, **141**
Klemmedson, Bob, **105**, 116, 150
Kopecky, Ray, 104, 117, 153
Krause, Edward, **13**
Kruger, Andy, **130**

LCI (landing craft, infantry), 87
LCM (landing craft, mechanized), **3**, 64
LCVP (landing craft, vehicle/personnel), 127
Liberty ships, 2, 66, 85
Lilly, Bill, **127**
Lipchutz, Doc, 52
LST (landing ship, tank), 38, 66, **82**, 83, 85, 86, 126, **126**, **139**, **141**, 143
Lyn, Capt. George O., **7**
Lynch, Jim, 20, 61, **62**, 73

MacArthur, Gen. Douglas, 38, 83, 98–99, 140
Macnaughton, C., 55
Manion, Charles, **149**, 163
Marston Mat, **94**

Masterson, Charles "Mickey," 12
McCraley, Tom, 20
McCrary, Jim, 102
Mead, Capt. Charles P., 52
Mexican Expeditionary Air Force (MEAF), 120, 121, 124
Mitchell, Gen. Billy, 28
Mitsubishi Raiden (Thunderbolt) J-2M3 (Jack), 148, **148**, 153
Moody, Charles L., 12
Mosquito (de Havilland), 76
Mulligan, Bob, 52

Nakajima KI-87, **147**
Nakajima KI-115 (Tsurgi Sword), **146**
Nance, Bethel, 130
Nevill, Ed, **53**
Nickell, Lt. Don, 20, **53**
Nicks (Japanese fighters), 96
19th Bombardment Squadron (Silver Fleet), 22d Bomber Group, 19, 21, 26
90th Bomber Group (Jolly Rogers), 75
9th Fighter Squadron (Flying Knights), 49th Fighter Group, 83, 90

110th Tactical Reconnaissance Squadron, 108
Otawari, Japanese airstrip at, 69

P-38 (Lockheed "Lightning"): decoration of, 110, 116, 117; in Japan, 136–38, **137**, 140, 161; maintenance of, 33; pride in, 34; in Southwest Pacific Area (SWPA), 31–34; at U.S. air bases, 19, **32**, 59, 61, 69, 90, **91**, 109, **110**, 119, 126, 129

P-39, 19

P-40 (Kittyhawk), 19, 28

P-40N, 81

P-47 (Thunderbolt), 91, 95, 98, 121

P-51 (Mustang), 108

P-61 (Black Widow), 93

P-70 (Douglas Havoc), 19, 56, 92

Pasadena, USS, 141

Patrol Craft 466, 140

PB4Y2 Privateer, 118

PBM (patrol bomber, Mariner), 66, 70

PBY (amphibious patrol bomber, Catalina), 69, 80, 121

Pipino, Roy, 56

P-V2 (Lockheed Harpoon), 98

Robey, John, 73

Rogers, George, 111

Scheid, Lt. Ray, 21, 66, 73

Searight, Lt. Bob, 90

2d Bombardment Squadron, 22d Bomber Group, 19

Seiders, Lieutenant, 127

7th Fighter Squadron (Screamin' Demons), 49th Fighter Group, 26, 90, 111; Communications Section, 107

Shelman, Jake, 127, 131

Sievers, Larry, 149, 150

Sikorsky R-4 helicopter, 112

Sisson, Sylvan, 111

Smith, Maj. Howard E., 52

Sonia (Japanese attacker), 68

Spindler, Don, 149

Spruell, George, Jr., 111

Supermarine Walrus, 56, 57

Swarts, Wayne K., 145

Sykora, Joseph, 13, 19, 25, 34, 34–36

Taylor, Herschel, 40, 53

Thirteenth Air Force, USAAF, 69

33d Bombardment Squadron, 22d Bomber Group, 19

33d Fighter Control Squadron: at Aihoma (Milne Bay), 11; at Cape Gloucester, 38–61; departure of and voyage overseas, 5–8; at Oro Bay, 18–21; at Sansapor, 66–67

Thomas, Hurschel, 53

305th Airdrome Squadron, 90

Tice, Lt. Col. Clay, 136–38, 137, 140

Tjisadane (Dutch merchant ship), 18

Tony fighters, 46–47, 138, 147

20th Combat Mapping Squadron, 75

22d Bomber Group (Red Raiders), 19, 21–22, 28, 31

201st Mexican Fighter Squadron, Mexican Expeditionary Air Force, 120, 121, 124

Venable, Vernel "Tex," 53

Watkins, Stanley, 53

Webster, George "Doc," 127, 153, 159

Wecker, Bob, 146, 149

Woodford, Ken, 48, 53

Zebrowski, Stanley F., 12

Zero, (Japanese fighter), 31, 95, 143